Letting People In

Letting People In

Tips & Stories From a BnB Host

Rochelle Short

Type A Seattle
Seattle, Washington

www.lettingpeoplein.com

Published by Type A Seattle

Copyright © 2014 by Rochelle Short

Cover Design and Art © 2014 by Michelle McCartney

Edited by Sara Addicott

Formatted by Bee Tangsurat

Author Photograph by Brady Wolf

First Edition: July 2014

ISBN-13: 978-0990572619

ISBN-10: 0990572617

To my mother, who taught me to read, and to my brother Mark, who grew up reading and writing alongside me.

TABLE OF CONTENTS

AUTHOR'S NOTE

Sometimes I watch people walk by on the street and think to myself, they could be the next guests sharing the wall of my third-floor bedroom.

Aided by the Internet, complete strangers from all over the globe come to stay in my home. I am a changed person because of their visits. In the following pages, I offer advice and stories from my first year as a host via the home-sharing website Airbnb.com. Every story is true, but names and identifying facts have been changed to protect the identities of my guests and friends.

LEAVING HOME

It was the dead of winter in 2013, and I was devastated from a gut-wrenching breakup that had happened in early December. Despite the many weeks that had passed, the pain was acute. I knew something needed to change, and I desperately wanted to get out of the house I had shared with my ex-boyfriend, Grayson. Too many reminders of our failed romance littered my home. I discovered that's the trouble with being the homeowner—he's gone, but you remain stuck with a mortgage under the same roof that holds all the memories.

I'd purchased my home in Seattle's tony Green Lake neighborhood ten years earlier. The area is coveted by many due to its proximity to the lake itself, which features a lush park and a highly trafficked 2.8 mile walking path where fashionistas, first-daters, and fitness buffs go to exercise and parade. When I bought the house during Seattle's prolonged housing boom of the early millennium, I envisioned an eventual husband and child occupying its two bedrooms with me.

They never materialized. The closest I'd come to marriage wasn't even that close—two successive live-in boyfriends who'd each lasted about six months before they fled our relationship. I have since come to the conclusion that I might not have been the easiest person to live with. You see, I used to be a bit of an emotionally high-maintenance person. Not to imply that the men were perfect gems, either. They'd both had failings of their own, as roommates and as partners, but in life I'd always sought out the perfectly imperfect.

These guys were notable in my life because they were the only people I ever lived with who weren't related to me. As you read my stories, perhaps you'll catch glimpses of why I spent a decade mostly alone in my 1,800-square-foot, 1929 brick bungalow.

When a call from Jeff, a former boyfriend—one who'd never lived with me—arrived, asking me for property management help, my curiosity was piqued. I was one of his few contacts in the Seattle real estate industry, and he knew I'd have advice to share about property management. I'd spent eleven years working as an office manager for a real estate brokerage firm in Seattle.

I've had lifelong fascination with real estate and the meaning of home. We moved so much—every two or three years—when I was a child and my dad was in the military. Though my family lived in a lot of houses, we never really had anything like a home of our own. When we finally left the protective arms of the military in the late 1980s, my parents settled in Phoenix, Arizona.

Wide-eyed, I looked around the flat neighborhoods and generously sized streets filled with terra-cotta-colored homes. A little culture-shocked to be back in the States, I cautiously regarded the one-story ramblers that were so different from the barracks-style housing we'd lived in during our recent, three-year assignment in Okinawa, Japan. Coming from the neutered blandness of a military base, the charming cul-de-sacs and backyard pools were a welcome and exciting change for a nine year old.

I remember being both intrigued and intimidated by the affable, elderly real estate broker in his mustard-yellow blazer who toured us around to various homes. Most of all, I remember my parents' secret code to one another about whether or not they liked a home we were visiting. It went like this: if one of them opened the oven door, this signaled the other person that they'd like to get the hell out of the house and on to the next property. My dad thought this secret procedure would expedite the process by removing the need to play pretend with the realtor, making my parents' decision to move on appear mutual.

Such a simple thing, really. Perhaps even a bit odd. But in my young mind, the world of real estate signaled weighty adult decisions and great possibility. In each new house we toured, I enjoyed fantasizing about how my little-girl life could unfold, and perhaps my grown-up life, too. Was this the house where I'd someday be visiting my aging parents and toting around a couple of toddlers who'd play in the kidney-shaped pool?

We eventually settled on a house with an oval-shaped pool, but my parents separated within the year. After the split, my mother took my brother and me north to Washington State where we have all lived ever since.

At the tender age of twenty-two, six months after graduating from the University of Washington, I paid off all my college loans and got my first real job. I was offered a killer salary to work six hours a day as a receptionist at an independent real estate office ten minutes north of downtown Seattle.

One day out of the blue, the veteran office manager of eighteen years unexpectedly gave notice. She'd decided to run off and marry a hunky stonemason fifteen years her junior. It was a blow to the owner, who had been her longtime friend; he considered her his best confidante. When the owner called me into his office to inform me of the manager's departure, I shakily walked in, sure I was about to be fired. I was shocked by the news of her resignation and even more surprised that I was being offered her job less than one year after being hired. This was an enormous promotion and the position carried a lot of responsibility. Stepping into her role ushered me into earning a six-figure salary. This came as a bit of a shock to a girl with a bachelor's degree in psychology who never expected to earn such a hefty sum in a year, or several successive years, truthfully.

By the age of twenty-three, I, alongside my broker, oversaw nearly one hundred real estate agents and three staff members. False bravado and a great poker face got me through the next ten years. Those years were the height of Seattle's thriving real estate heyday, which ultimately proved to be too financially lax. Lenders were giving out loans far above what borrowers' incomes could support. Self-employed people were claiming inflated income, but few underwriters were actually checking to ensure income claims were true. And no-down, or low-down payments were rampant. It seemed everyone was casually buying homes, and watching this happen all around me spurred me to purchase my own home two months after I turned twenty-six.

Real estate was booming...until it wasn't. Late in 2010, with Seattle deep in the throes of the Great Recession, I looked around my quiet office and woefully regarded my still-robust paycheck. The owner of my company was extremely generous and paid his staff far above the market rate for our work, even during the economic downturn. But I'd begun to feel that the money wasn't enough. In my soul, I knew it was time for a career change. I was bored by the daily tasks that were no longer fulfilling or intellectually challenging. I wanted to write, or at least work in a creative field. I knew if I went back to school, or "followed my bliss" as Joseph Campbell so wisely encouraged people to do, the gap in my resume could be explained by the depressed economy.

Bolstering my courage to ask to be laid off from the only job I'd had since college, I fantasized about new endeavors and comforted myself by envisioning my future interviewer. "Ms. Short, I see a gap in your resume from 2010-2012." The man (he was always a man) would shuffle my anemic resume around on his desk, looking bored. Until the pause. "Oh...I see you worked in the real estate industry when the housing bubble burst. Never mind." Case closed. The national financial crisis was my get-out-of-mental-jail-free card, and I was hell-bent on using it.

During my tenure at the company, I learned a lot about the neighborhoods of Seattle and the contract process of buying and selling a home. I also met a lot of great clients and real estate agents. But it felt like the right time to close that chapter of my life.

In the immediate months following my departure, instead of pursuing my bliss or studying for the GRE, I spent a lot of time drinking at happy hours and hanging out with other unemployed people. It was not a productive time, but in my heart I knew I needed the break from the constant obligations that had kept me running—since kindergarten, it seemed—like a high-functioning hamster on a wheel.

In a bout of inspiration, and with a desire to escape feeling pressure to figure out my next professional move, I thought it wise to throw myself into online dating. Since I had so much free time on my hands, husband-chasing seemed like a great full-time gig until I identified my true calling. 'Cause really, what screams desirability more than an out-of-work woman with no immediate professional goals or prospects on the horizon?

A few months into my entertaining forays into online dating, I met a scientist named Jeff. He had just turned forty and seemed excited (like they always are at first) to date me. We fell in like that spring, never professing "I love you" to one another, and our relationship only lasted until early December.

Have you noticed that my breakups tend to occur in early December? Odder still, both successive relationships met their demise on the eighth of December! I quickly came to the conclusion that the Universe was trying to teach me a couple of important things: 1) Don't date men whose middle names are William, and 2) Leave town—alone—on December 8th.

I had not spoken to Jeff during the year I'd spent meeting, falling head over heels in love with, cohabitating with, and ultimately being left by Grayson, who was the cause of my 2013 winter depression. But Jeff trusted my real estate knowledge and wanted my advice. He asked me to dinner, and pre-empted the invitation by saying he was looking for a property management company to oversee his Capitol Hill townhome in his absence, because his job demanded that he work out of state for a few years.

In the early months of 2013, the Seattle real estate market was starting to show signs of life, well ahead of the rest of the nation. This resurgence was likely due to the fact that major employers like Starbucks, Costco, and the behemoth Amazon are all headquartered in the Emerald City. Despite the market picking up, Jeff's townhome had not yet reached a value that made it worth selling, and he thought that renting the place would be a smart financial decision. He'd reconsider selling after the national and local economies improved.

Jeff and I met for dinner, and over beers and pub food, we made small talk and caught up. Eventually we got around to the subject of his house and the reason for our dinner. Wanting to be helpful and to appear as knowledgeable about the market as he'd believed me to be, I made a feeble attempt to search on my iPhone for a property manager I'd known during my real estate days. I couldn't find her information and told him that perhaps her business hadn't survived the recession.

We finished our meal, and Jeff walked me to my car. After a stiff hug, I promised I'd get back to him with more referrals once I reached out to my wide network of real estate agents. Thankfully, many were still my friends even though we no longer worked together.

I returned home that evening and sought comfort in the bed where I'd recently spent an embarrassing amount of hours wallowing in the depths of romantic and career-related despair. That night, however, instead of returning to the ever-familiar dark companion of hopelessness, I noticed an ember of possibility was coming to life inside of me.

I knew what I had to do. It scared the hell out of me, but I knew it was time.

THE LIFELINE

The next day, instead of calling my real estate contacts and tracking down active property managers, I looked around my too-small, too-lonely, too-depressing home and called Jeff. I told him I wanted to rent his three-bedroom, three-bath townhouse while he was away. But I had one important condition: he'd have to allow me to rent rooms to travelers through the online travel marketplace for hosts and guests called Airbnb.com.

I first learned of Airbnb while ghostwriting for a freelance photographer I'd met in the winter of 2012. Annie was a wedding and corporate events photographer, and when her business slowed during the recession, she started renting two of the three bedrooms in her North Seattle home through Airbnb. Because of the erratic nature of freelance work (with which I was acutely familiar when we met), Annie wanted extra income to ensure she could comfortably pay her monthly mortgage.

Since its inception in 2008, Airbnb has provided everyday folks around the world a way to list extra rooms in their homes. Usually the rooms are in typical homes and apartments, but people also offer quirky lodging options like castles, treehouses, tents, and Airstream trailers.

The company name came from an experience two of the three co-founders, Brian Chesky and Joe Gebbia, had in October of 2007 while living in San Francisco. As designers who often struggled to pay their rent, they'd noticed that an international design conference in town had filled up most of the city's hotel rooms. Hoping to make a little extra cash that weekend, the gentlemen blew up a few air mattresses and built a website overnight that offered last-minute conference attendees who still needed lodging a chance to stay in their "air bed and breakfast."

Three guests of varying ages—a man from India, a woman from Boston, and a man from Idaho—happily showed up and paid for the privilege of sleeping on the air mattresses in their home. Chesky and Gebbia observed that not only were the three guests intrigued by the website and the home-sharing concept, they were thrilled to have the opportunity to stay in a local's apartment. That spur-of-the-moment weekend experiment planted the seed for what is today a multi-billion-dollar company.

Unlike other free, home-sharing sites like couchsurfers.com, hosts on Airbnb charge a nightly lodging fee. Guests pay the rate, plus cleaning fees and an additional service fee to Airbnb. It's free for hosts to list their space, but they do pay a small percentage of the overall booking price to cover the credit card processing fee that the company incurs while facilitating the transaction.

In the nascent days of the company, when the co-founders were the primary users of the site—both as hosts and as guests in others' homes—they experienced firsthand the uncomfortable aspect of dealing with cash transactions. To eliminate the awkwardness of guests and hosts exchanging money in person, they revised the terms so that Airbnb now processes a guest's credit card when a reservation is confirmed. Airbnb holds the money until 24 hours after a guest successfully checks in, and then makes a direct deposit into the host's checking account. Everything is above board, and at the end of the tax year, Airbnb sends the host a 1099 statement of their earnings to file with the IRS.

ANNIE

I met Annie a few months after I began the certificate program in editing at the University of Washington. That prior summer, after months of being a professional barfly and an aimless depressive, I decided it was time to get off my barstool and return to the classroom. I enrolled in the program and went to my first class in October. Nine months later, I graduated, certificate in hand. Editing was a natural transition for me, because in my heart of hearts, I wasn't yet confident enough to pursue a writing career.

Writing has been a passion of mine since I was a little girl. Lacking the discipline and education I felt was required to become a professional writer, I'd spent much of my professional career wielding my red pen on other people's work. Editing documents, both at the office and for friends, had become a runner-up to actually having the guts to write for myself. Because of the recent boom in self-publishing, I saw getting my editor accreditation as a great career move, especially since it didn't require spending two years in pursuit of a master's degree.

While acquiring my editing certificate, I supplemented my meager income with small writing gigs and freelance work doing floral designs (one of the many ways I put myself through college), but these jobs paid just above minimum wage. Through a floral designer I worked wedding and gala events with, I met Annie. An experienced documentary photographer, Annie had mastered the visuals on her website, but needed a wordsmith to help market her brand. She hired me to write blog articles and help her with social media.

One unusually bright winter morning, while Annie and I were working together on an article at her dining table, I heard heavy footfalls ascending her stairs. I knew Annie was single, so I was surprised to hear a man calling out a greeting to her as he approached the living room's second-floor landing. At the top of the stairs, her two Yorkshire Terriers circled him excitedly and amicably, implying they knew him well.

A landscaper from Arizona, Annie's visitor had decided to spend the winter months trying out a change of scenery in lush, verdant Seattle. According to Annie, he'd already set up shop here, and his business was booming in the wealthy neighborhoods that lined Puget Sound. After initially booking a one-month stay at Annie's place via Airbnb, he had extended his stay for several months and didn't seem to be leaving any time soon. I was surprised to hear that until he arrived, they'd been total strangers. But I was also very intrigued. Due to the casual nature of our professional relationship, as soon as he was out of earshot, I peppered Annie with questions about her experience as a host.

Was she worried about safety? Without asking for explicit details, was the income enough to make it worth the risk and efforts required to keep her home clean for guests? Did she have any bad experiences? Who were her favorite guests? As she patiently answered all my questions a seed was planted in my mind.

When I told Jeff about my decision to host on Airbnb—if he'd allow me to rent his gorgeously appointed, centrally located home, that is—I assured him he was welcome to visit anytime. Since enough time had passed since our breakup, and I'd learned about a deeper level of romantic connection from dating Grayson, I knew I would never be tempted to date Jeff again.

The night I met Grayson, a man sitting at the bar a few

stools down from us looked at us and asked me how long we'd been together. We'd been on our first date for barely an hour, but our level of attraction and comfort with one another was obvious and palpable. That man—and numerous friends for months afterward—said they enjoyed watching us together. Falling in love with Grayson was swift and effortless. It was heady and intoxicating and unmoored me from myself. I'd never felt anything like it. I loved Grayson deeply, and for a time, he claimed to also love me. Since Jeff and I had never felt love toward, nor exchanged words of love with, one another, it was easy to see him as only a friend. If Jeff someday chose to return to Seattle for a visit, it wouldn't be weird to have him stay in my/his home.

Jeff has always been a fairly laid-back individual, so he took the Airbnb request and invitation to return anytime in stride. I think he was simply relieved that I'd be living in his home instead of strangers. Jeff knew I would take care of the place, and he gave me his blessing.

My wish for change had been answered.

Energized by the prospect of my new life and the chance to escape my house and the memories associated with it, I sprang into action. I booked a lunch date with Annie to consult with her about the specific ins and outs of Airbnb, chatted with my accountant, secured tenants for my Green Lake house, and prepared to pack for the five-mile move across town.

NEW BEGINNINGS

February to April was a flurry of excitement and exhaustion. While I was at my Green Lake bungalow packing up my belongings, donating childhood stuffed animals, and ditching the street discards I'd hoped to one day refurbish, contractors were busy at Jeff's townhome. He'd already moved out of state, but had given me a generous budget to refinish the hardwoods, repaint any rooms that needed a fresh coat on the walls, and replace the pet-stained carpets.

Before the truck arrived to move Jeff two states away, I photographed the third-floor and entry-floor rooms of house and listed them on Airbnb. This was just a "starter" listing that I would eventually update with new photos once my possessions were in the home. I knew it was vitally important to list the rooms as soon as possible because I hoped to have my first guests lined up when I moved in on April 1st. And just as I'd planned, within days of posting my listing, I had my first request for a booking. This felt like a good omen. I thought, *maybe I can really do this!*

At 1:30 in the morning, my phone jolted me awake with an alert from Airbnb. Isabella, an American expat living in Italy with her son, wanted to stay with me in late August. I guess I'd unknowingly signed up to receive push notifications from the site and had never given an ounce of thought to the time zones of my potential guests. More jarring than the sudden middle of the night awakening, was the shocking realization someone half a world away had been looking at my place!

As I cautiously stepped into my role as a BnB host, I wondered if receiving alerts at all hours from guests around the world was going to be my new normal. Should I reply to them during my night, which was their day, or would that look too desperate? I worried if I would ever sleep through the night again. Clearly I had to set some parameters for myself.

I accepted Isabella's request for a summer stay and promptly turned off the push notifications. If I were going to let people into my home, it would be on my terms, and not at a frenetic pace. I did not want to appear as if I were dying for the income and needed my life to revolve around this new venture. Though truthfully, to some extent, it really did.

I graduated from my editing program in June of 2012, and when I moved into the townhouse the spring of 2013, I was slowly gaining traction in my new freelance career. Because I'd spent a lot of time on Facebook, Instagram, and Twitter during my slothful days of unemployment, I'd become a bit of a social media "guru" and was able to market my new skills to clients. Being able to write, spell, use semicolons correctly, and craft an occasional story was proving to be a marketable asset. Seattle businesses were slowly, but assuredly, crawling out of the hole that the recession had created.

At the time of the move, I was also editing my first book project, a memoir by a cast member of *The Real Housewives of Atlanta* and her husband. How their publisher found me is a long and karmic story, but the acclaim of editing a book for a reality TV star was worth more than the money I earned from the gig. It also assured me the Universe had my back and that there was still money to be made in book publishing.

My various writing, editing, and social media gigs were keeping me busy around the clock, but were still not paying all my bills. To gain confidence and traction with my new roster of freelance clientele, I charged lower rates while I essentially interned for myself, learning a ton of new skills in a short time. Hosting on Airbnb came at a time that I, and so many others like me, desperately needed a financial lifeline to aid us through the recession.

I remember sitting at my computer watching Airbnb promotional videos after I first posted my listings. I teared up at footage of empty-nesters and single moms who were effectively using their extra space to connect with world travelers while trying to make a better life for themselves in the process. I was warmed watching footage of a dignified man in India fluffing pillows, setting out fresh flowers, and writing a welcome card for his soon-to-arrive guests. I wanted to be like him. I took notes while checking out the site's hospitality tips. A longtime people-pleaser, I felt confident I would excel as a BnB host.

Airbnb relies on reviews from guests and hosts to evaluate their experiences with one another. The reviews serve as an endorsement (or warning) to both hosts and guests. I find they are essential to keep in mind when reaching out to make a reservation or deciding whether to accept a reservation request. Peer reviews and experiential reviews are designed to offer transparency about both guests and hosts and also to put faces to the people who use the site globally.

In addition to promoting the obvious financial value of using the site, Airbnb has a strong desire to convey the intangible value of connecting with real people, with the hope of promoting a sense of community among its users. From the beginning, Airbnb set itself apart from other home-sharing sites like couchsurfers.com and Craigslist .com because their site focuses on the connection between the host *and* the home, rather than just the host *or* the home.

When I first listed my rooms, I had no reviews, so I

asked Annie to write me a reference. Airbnb allows fellow hosts to write peer reviews if they know you personally— even if they haven't actually stayed in your home. In her statement about me, Annie wrote that she'd rarely encountered a person so eager to make those around her happy, and that I was extremely attentive to others' needs. I guess she'd caught on to the fact that I was a bit of a people-pleaser.

When it comes to hospitality, people-pleasing is an asset. So is having a keen attention to detail (hello, editor!) and being able to skillfully wield a rag. As a teenager, I cleaned professionally with my mom after tenants had moved out of their apartments. Rental clean-outs are one of the most taxing and difficult jobs in the cleaning industry, so at a very young age, I learned a standard of cleanliness that has served me well as a host.

Though it often takes me an hour to clean a room, I only charge guests a $15 cleaning fee. It seems reasonable to me, and effectively pays me minimum wage and covers the cost of laundering the room's linens. For people considering becoming hosts, ask yourself: 1) How much do you like to clean? 2) What is your standard of cleanliness and will it exceed your guests' standards? 3) Are you willing to hire a cleaning service if you're not up to the task of cleaning your own place?

These are very important questions to consider. Really knowing what your standards are and what you're capable of is essential before deciding what to charge for cleaning—or deciding to hire someone to do it for you. When traveling, do you like finding a stray pubic hair on your sheets or in the bathtub? Yeah, I don't either. After I clean and do the final walk-through of a room, I pretend I am visiting a strange hotel room for the first time. This level of detail comes naturally to me, but everyone is different.

When I recently used Airbnb to book summer accommodations in New York City, I saw cleaning rates as high as $75 per booking. In that highly sought-after metropolis, it's not unusual for hosts to state that guests must pay the cleaning fee in cash upon arrival. I imagine (and hope) that this cash fee goes directly to their cleaning person. This fee—which can and does vary widely—is an additional factor to consider, both as a host when you're setting your rate and as a guest when you're considering a reservation, because it's on top of the nightly rate, and so is the service fee.

For my initial nightly rate, I charged a very low fee of $69 a night for my first few months of business. This was bargain-basement pricing, considering the close proximity of my townhouse to the downtown core and tourist attractions. April was still the off-season for Seattle tourism, and I simply wanted to get people in the door so I could pay my rent and pile up some reviews on the site to boost my appeal. I felt like a crack dealer. Lure 'em in cheap and get 'em hooked on the product so they'll tell other people.

My ploy worked, and soon I had more requests to stay than I had rooms to offer.

FIRST GUESTS

Within two days of moving in, my first guests arrived. A French couple living in New York City decided to visit Seattle on a whim, hence their last-minute request for a reservation. As I sat in a coffee shop pretending to work on a client's social media—but actually spending too much time on personal social media—I saw their message arrive via Airbnb. They'd just arrived in town and wondered if they could stay for two nights.

After an initial moment of excitement, I was beside myself with fear. But the terror I felt was thankfully accompanied by the half realization, half confirmation that this gig could actually work out. Utilizing the site's messaging platform, I quickly contacted the pair and told them yes, I did have a room, so long as they didn't mind stepping around a few moving boxes.

Airbnb's platform allows hosts and potential guests to chat back and forth but not exchange email addresses or see phone numbers until a reservation is confirmed. If they've both entered their phone numbers, they may call via the site's in-house connect service to speak with one another before confirming a reservation. Understandably, from a fiscal and security standpoint, Airbnb likes to monitor all communication between parties. This also protects the identities of both host and guest before an actual reservation is made.

To expedite the messaging process, the site has implemented an "Instant Book" feature that encourages hosts turn on a setting that allows guests to book instantly without communicating with the host. This might be a great feature if you're a host who does not live at the property and therefore may not care as much who you're renting to. Personally, I prefer to screen my guests via messaging and occasional phone calls, so I do not use this setting.

As a woman who lives alone, I consider the option to refuse a reservation to be invaluable. I won't confirm a booking with a guest unless I have messaged them, read their reviews (if they have any), and gotten a sense they're a decent person—as much as you can get a sense about someone after a few emails and a photo or two. A girl's gotta have her standards, and I need to feel safe.

The French pair from NYC assured me the moving boxes would be no problem and confirmed the reservation. In that moment at the coffee shop, I finally felt like I was officially in business. It was the first tangible confirmation I'd received since deciding to move that making a major change to my life was actually possible. Going through the motions of photographing the rooms, entering the listing, and crossing my fingers that people would like what I had to offer was all prep work. Once all that was in order, my life was suspended while I waited, with bated breath, to see if people would actually click on my rooms and book a stay.

Welcoming that couple through the door and accepting their payment was proof positive that success was at my fingertips, as long as I was willing to work hard, stretch outside my comfort zone…and most of all, believe in myself and my abilities.

I took a deep breath, gave myself a mental high five, and opened the front door.

THE BURLY GERMAN

Immediately after the French couple left (after a two-night stay that went off without a hitch), their third-floor room was booked by an affable-looking, young German man. Since I worked from home, I was there to greet him when he arrived.

My presence wasn't technically necessary, as I'd I installed a push-button, key-code box on my front door so guests could access my home without a key whenever they needed to. Each guest is assigned a personal number that I delete after their visit. This way, I don't have to plan my days and evenings around their check-in and saves both me and my guests a bunch of hassle. It also allows me to sleep through the night if they arrive late.

My stated check-in time is any time after 3:00 p.m., and guests must check out by 11:00 a.m. The Schlage coded key box was the best business purchase I ever made, and I can't imagine running this business without it. Various models in different colors and button styles are available at big box hardware stores and online for around $120.

When I opened the door to greet the young German, I was taken aback by his sheer size. He was huge—much larger than he looked in his profile photo. In that moment, it became clear that this was my first test of whether I could feel safe in my home with an unknown man—and in this case, a very large one—sleeping down the hall. When I told my mother I'd be moving across town and hosting strangers in my house, she was justifiably alarmed. With bravado, and desperation for change, I assured her I'd be fine.

For my safety, as well as to provide security for guests' belongings, I made sure that all the bedrooms in the house had secure doors that locked internally and came with private keys. I also told my mom I'd keep weapons in my room if it made her feel better. It didn't, and I didn't. Unless you count the Swiss Army knife and mace I often forget I have in my nightstand.

Another great safety tip I picked up from travel blogger Jodi Ettenberg of Legal Nomads was to use a rubber door stopper to ward off would-be assailants. Once you stick the handy rubber wedge under the doorframe, intruders are presumably kept at bay. For a mere $1.50 at the hardware store, I procured a brown wedge and promptly installed it under my door every night. My mother's fears were not assuaged. She was convinced I'd be raped in my sleep. Or burglarized, or meet some other nefarious fate. I did what I could.

Another great thing about hosting through Airbnb is their million-dollar Host Guarantee. When I first considered hosting, Annie gave me a little of the backstory about what had prompted Airbnb to offer this comforting insurance (of sorts).

In June of 2011, a San Francisco host returned home after a trip abroad to find her house had been burglarized and ransacked by her Airbnb guest, "Dj Patterson", who had been there one week. The host didn't know if the guest was a man or woman, but during the course of the booking, she had received a number of amiable emails, in which "Dj" had raved about the place. But in reality, "Dj," and his or her likely accomplices, had caused thousands of dollars' worth of damage to the San Francisco woman's home. They'd also cut into the walls and stolen priceless heirlooms out of her safe.

The host was understandably incensed. She felt that since Airbnb was charging her a fee, it was their job to properly verify the identity of the clientele they sent into people's homes. She claimed that when she used a no-fee site like Craigslist.com, she was repeatedly warned she was using the community-based site at her own risk. At the time of the San Francisco incident, Airbnb offered no such warning on their site.

After initially handling the situation poorly, Airbnb did an about face in August of 2011, and offered an unprecedented $50,000 guarantee to any host whose home sustained damage as a result of a guest. According to Annie, Airbnb also sent photos of the San Francisco crime scene to all the hosts on their site, alerting them to the issue and informing them of the steps the company was taking to ensure host safety.

In May of 2012, due to rapid growth (and presumably, deeper coffers), Airbnb secured insurance underwritten by Lloyd's of London which upped the $50,000 Host Guarantee to its current protection of up to one million dollars. If a host sustains damage to their home as a direct result of a guest's visit, the host can make a claim with Airbnb. The guarantee doesn't cover all countries, nor does it cover things like rare artwork, jewelry, and pets. A host must still purchase homeowner's or renter's insurance, but the Host Guarantee allows hosts like Annie and me to feel financially comforted beyond normal insurance when we open our doors to strangers.

SHARING

By the end of my robust first month of hosting, I discovered, with some surprise, that I was enjoying my interactions with guests a lot more than I'd expected. Friends and family were some of my early supporters and were happy to promote and share my listings with their friends and coworkers. But although they were willing to help spread the word, I sensed many of my friends and family still felt a little nervous about my new venture. Naturally, at the time, so was I.

The home-sharing concept of Airbnb was, and still is, fairly new to most people. When I mention it in conversation, about half the people I talk to are familiar with the site. I always pause after I say the name once to look for a flicker of recognition to cross the face of the person I am speaking with. If they give me a blank stare, I say the name again slowly and tell them a little about the site and how it works. Just like I was when I first saw Annie's situation, people seem to be endlessly curious about my experience allowing complete strangers into my home.

After a few weeks of hosting, I soon grew tired of telling the same stories at dinner parties and assuaging people's constant fears about my safety. In an effort to combat the fatigue of repeat storytelling, and to try to alleviate my friends' fears, I started sharing tidbits of my experiences on Facebook.

In my Facebook posts, I never identified guests by name. I would, however, mention their age, relationship to their travel companion, where they were from, and their gender—if it was relevant to my story. Because of the sharing nature of Facebook—it offers the ability to casually peek into one another's lives in as polished or as casual a way as one likes—the posts grew in popularity. Even the Facebook voyeurs who weren't overtly "liking" my status updates were approaching me at parties or messaging me privately to tell me how much they liked reading about my guests.

My intent with these Facebook stories was not to expose or embarrass people or to sensationalize any experiences I had with guests. Interacting with my guests allowed me glimpses into other cultures, and offered me both a way to reflect on the life choices I'd already made and an opportunity to ponder the way I wanted to live my life moving forward. I put these experiences into words because I felt it important to share with my friends my belief that we should not fear the world beyond our personal spaces or people in nearby states and far-flung countries.

The idea for this book came when I began doing free, in-home consultations for friends interested in becoming hosts. I noticed I got a lot of the same questions over and over, and I found myself repeatedly offering the same advice. I thought some of my tips about hosting could be helpful to those who were considering sharing space in their homes. And for those not among my limited sphere on Facebook, I thought the stories might be entertaining and unique, with particular appeal to folks who love to travel.

I am not a blogger, though I ghostwrite for others and am a freelance copy writer. The blogosphere is full of wonderful writers, and I admire their energy and stamina in connecting with their readers. At one point, I considered starting a blog where I would post updates as interesting exchanges happened in my home. However, I decided not to publicly share stories on the Internet about my guests until I got some internal clarity about why I was writing the stories. I also wanted to protect both my identity and theirs.

Using Facebook was a comfortable way to limit my audience and to gauge people's interest in my experiences. The stories included in this book have been expanded from those original Facebook posts. Due to the limited attention spans of readers on social media, for my original posts, I tried to limit the word count to fewer than 500 words each. But in this book, I'm able to reveal things I wasn't comfortable sharing when I first started writing about my journey as a host. The dates remain intact because some were seasonally relevant.

I hope these stories offer value or make you think. Perhaps the tales and tips from my first year as a host will encourage you to open your own door to strangers. Perhaps not. At the end of the day, I'd love it if you walk away with a sense that most people in this world are decent, kind folks—just like you. When you regard a stranger on the bus, or sidle up beside someone at the next barstool, I encourage you to look for your similarities with them rather than your differences. Maybe you'll even say hello.

By opening up my home, I've opened up my eyes…and my heart. In the past year, some guests have become fuzzy memories recalled only when I saw their names in my ledger at tax time. Other guests were teachers, offering me lessons I didn't realize I needed to learn. And the best ones? They became friends.

Would you like to meet some of them?

SPRING

My current guests are a married couple in their seventies reuniting stateside with their son, a documentary filmmaker. The son works for a D.C. think tank and arrived in Seattle after spending several months working on an extensive project in Somalia. His sturdy, black travel containers filled with film equipment fill my entire foyer. It feels exciting to walk into my house, like I am on the set of a National Geographic shoot or some other informative, ground-breaking work destined to educate the masses.

The son is cute and youngish, probably in his early thirties. Blonde hair, blue eyes, and an athletic physique. He's the kind of person I'd be thrilled to meet at a party and chat with all night, hoping we'd eventually exchange numbers.

It still unsettles me that if I wanted to, I could simply walk downstairs in my pajamas and chat with him in front of the fireplace in the comfort of my living room. A complete stranger! And a hot one at that! I didn't expect my first month of hosting to offer such delicious eye candy. From the mother, I learned that sadly, her handsome son has a wife. Even if he were single, I've set a personal rule for myself never to sleep with or attempt to seduce a guest. At least, that's the goal, and not mixing business with pleasure seems like a good idea.

The mom has always stayed in hotels, but her son has used Airbnb for years. In his calls to her from Somalia, he encouraged his folks to use the site. I am learning that you can often tell how travel-savvy people are by their familiarity with Airbnb. The son would have booked their lodging through his Airbnb account, but due to the remoteness and lack of Internet on his Somalian film location, he'd been unable to secure rooms in advance of his return to the States.

The mother followed her son's advice to try the site and messaged me several times to arrange their stay. She was nervous and unsure if she was booking the room correctly because the Airbnb platform was completely foreign to her. Unlike picking up a phone or using the Internet to secure a hotel room, the Airbnb site demands a few identity verifications and a couple more booking steps from its users. I admired the mother's moxie and her ability to tackle a new and unfamiliar concept. Eventually, she successfully confirmed their reservation for both of my rooms.

A week prior to their arrival, I began receiving more messages from the nervous mother. In one of the lengthy emails, she asked if I used (or could use) allergen-free laundry detergent on her towels and sheets. Her request gave me pause. I wondered what she did when she stayed in a traditional hotel. Do entirely chemical-free hotels even exist?

I briefly flirted with the idea of establishing parameters on how much I'd be willing to accommodate my guests' special needs. But I was now an active player in the hospitality industry, where one must be prepared for any request, so I thought it best to make such decisions on a case-by-case basis. I considered refusing her request, but decided against it after considering how I'd want someone to treat me if I were in the same situation.

Because of my wish to please and my desire to provide for her comfort, I trotted down to the local grocery and picked up some allergen-free detergent. She was thrilled by my willingness to accommodate her request, and I felt like a hero—all because of a five-dollar bag of special soap.

In business and in life, they say it's the little things that count. I am inclined to agree. My new life as a host surprises and challenges me daily, and I wouldn't have it any other way.

JEFF

4.28.13

It's the final weekend of my first month hosting, and the house is full. Under my roof? Two German women in their early thirties…and my ex, Jeff.

One of the women currently lives outside of Frankfurt and the other has recently moved to Maryland. Old friends who wanted to reunite in a location neither of them had ever visited, they chose Seattle because it was a good launching point for their planned road trip out to the Olympic National Park. They were also curious to see to see how the West Coast compared to the East Coast.

Jeff's relocation package included a paid trip back to Seattle within six months of his move, to allow him to "take care of his affairs." He thought it wise to take advantage of the free trip, and also wanted to see all the improvements the contractors had made to his place under my supervision.

I won't deny that it was strange coming home to what was now, according to the lease, *my* home. It had been the place where Jeff and I had spent most of our time together when we were dating. When I arrived home and reached the first floor—where the kitchen, dining area, and living room are situated—it was really weird to see Jeff sprawled out on my brown leather couch instead of his tattered beige one.

Despite my nervousness about the unique situation we now found ourselves in, I took a deep breath, grabbed two beers from the fridge, and offered him one. Friends thought I was crazy for renting Jeff's townhouse. Many of them admonished me for being kind to him even though we'd split up under less than ideal circumstances. Essentially, I walked out of his house one day after a huge fight and he never came after me. Jeff had accused me of being a drama queen and in response I'd told him he was emotionally neutered. It wasn't the first time we'd fought, but I'd always been the one to return with an attempt to make amends. That last fight and emotionally charged waiting game afterward was my test to see if he cared about me; his lack of pursuit confirmed to me that he did not.

In recent months, I sensed those same friends thought the only thing more insane than me renting from Jeff was me opening my door to complete strangers. I was still growing accustomed to what my new living situation meant for my identity and still had some nervousness about how I was perceived by others. Adding Jeff's physical presence into the mix only exacerbated my inner turmoil.

Sipping our beers awkwardly, we made small talk about his new job and he congratulated me on the way the house looked. He said he loved the improvements and the new way I'd laid out the living and dining rooms. Wanting to remind him of the practicalities of staying in a house that was now designed for Airbnb guests, I sheepishly warned him that my German guests might be arriving at the house any moment. I did this, in part, because of his position on the couch, and also because I wanted him to be prepared and not feel uncomfortable or act awkwardly toward my guests. I was growing accustomed to strangers walking into my home, but I didn't necessarily expect others to embrace the situation as readily.

A scientist and experienced world traveler, Jeff is an endlessly curious and adaptable person. His curiosity was one of his attributes that attracted me to him in the first place. But what didn't sit well with me when we were together was his curiosity about other women. Even then, I had to check a little lingering jealously when he seemed a little too excited to meet the two women who were about to arrive.

The German ladies showed up at the townhouse a half hour after I did. Once they deposited their bags in the upstairs room, they came downstairs to chat with the two of us in the living room. They seemed a little surprised when we explained we were exes, but that Jeff had moved away and I was now running the place. When I tell guests the story of how the house and Airbnb situation came to be, I get the sense that they imagine a big blow-up fight with Jeff storming out. And that I, the woman left behind, had at least gotten custody of the house. Which, of course, was not the case, but makes good fodder for suggestive storytelling.

I offered the ladies a beer and they filled us in on their day. While they entertained us with stories about their experiences in America, Jeff remained sprawled out on the couch like he owned the place (which he technically did).

Their gushing observations about Americans? We're a friendly lot. People in the U.S. are extremely outgoing and always seem willing to chat. "To make a bridge," one of the women said in stilted English and a gesture of hands—fingertips touching fingertips in an arc. Jeff spoke about his experiences in Germany and with Germans when he backpacked through Europe in his twenties. It was interesting to hear stories he'd never shared with me when we were dating. Eventually, the three of them started talking about politics.

Quietly removing myself from the fray of political conversation, I sat still in the corner, watching the scene unfold. Like the oft-fantasized-about fly on the wall, I took in the surreal scene of two gorgeous, intelligent women talking to my ex-boyfriend in a house I was now paying him to live in.

My life had taken a most interesting turn.

I was used to being the traveler, venturing out to exotic countries and sampling the culture, the food, and meeting the locals. Forever the military brat, comfortable in any location, I was endlessly optimistic about life's potential "out there." However, I'd now invited the world in, and folks from all over had accepted the invitation. It was amazing—I was getting to travel without leaving my house.

Eventually we said goodnight, and Jeff retired to the entry-floor room that had formerly been his office. Up in their bedroom, the women giggled and caught up with one another until the early hours of the morning. I, alone in my room on the same floor, listened to their laughter and reminisced about the pleasures of traveling with a best friend.

FINLAND

5.2.13

The house was full on May Day. Two women—a Canadian and a Finn—occupied the third-floor room. A couple checked out of the ground-floor room this morning, but I never met them in person. It's the second time in a month this has happened, and though I was alarmed the first time, I've adjusted to the idea. Because the key box makes it so easy for guests to come and go, I may not always meet them personally. This was a good practice in learning to let go. I needed to trust that people would be fine without me hovering or worrying if they're comfortable or having a nice time.

People always find it fascinating (and alarming) that I allow strangers into my home. I would never dare to tell them that sometimes I don't even see my guests if they code their way in and don't make a point to introduce themselves. I figure some people are shy, and I respect that and give them space. I never knock on people's bedroom doors for fear of disturbing their nap or "private" time; I introduce myself only if I see them in the common spaces, bump into them at the door, or if they text me to see if I am home or otherwise seek me out.

I think this fear of letting strangers into our interior spaces is kind of odd, since the boarding room concept has been around for ages. Think of all the novels you've read and films you've seen where the old widow runs a boarding house, or "lets rooms" for transient strangers who show up on her doorstep with nowhere to go. In the days before criminal background checks for tenants—and a 24-hour news cycle that has instilled a generalized fear in people—folks in society generally trusted one another.

I am not a Pollyanna, or so cavalier as to think something bad won't ever happen to me, but I refuse to live my life in fear like I'm living under a rock. I was the little girl who grew up with a mom who constantly warned her about men in vans offering candy to children, scaring the crap out of me while she was trying to protect me. The anxiety of my childhood, coupled with crippling shyness and a fear of strangers, was a way of living I was determined to leave behind.

Seven years of retail work and eleven years of having a steady stream of people in the foyer of my real estate office forced me to interact with strangers and to overcome some of my shyness. I eventually caught on to the fact that people are pretty decent. Nice, even, at least most of the time. The bulk of us muddle through our days with our fears, insecurities, and anxieties on our shoulders, striving to overcome them with accomplishments, love, and hope. I try to remind myself of this every day, especially when I am interacting with someone new. Everyone is afraid of something.

The mystery couple who stayed in the ground-floor room left me a sweet note and bottle of wine, so I guess they had a nice time in my home. Guests have left me expensive chocolates, wine, six packs of beer, and gift cards for coffee. When I find some sweet token left in the room for me, it feels like a cross between a maid's gratuity and a host thank-you gift. It's one more facet of this hosting gig that is totally unexpected, but heartwarming. I spent the morning cleaning the mystery guests' room, laundering their sheets, and thinking about the hotbed of activity the evening before.

It's become common in Seattle for anarchists to take

to the streets of Capitol Hill and downtown on May Day to protest global business injustices and poor working conditions.

Coming from my former house in sleepy Green Lake, it's refreshing to be in a neighborhood where newsworthy events occur just down the road. While helicopters buzzed loudly over my neighborhood for most of the evening, I calmly shared cups of chamomile tea with the Canadian and Finn in the kitchen.

The Finn inquired about the rows of bicycle cops the pair had seen earlier that evening as the Capitol Hill protest on Pike and Broadway was getting underway.

"Are the bikes a peaceful gesture initiated by the police to not incite violence?"

"Perhaps," I said, never having really thought about it, but now thinking maybe she was onto something.

"Hmmm. In Finland, cops just show up with horses, because nobody's gonna stone a horse."

MONTREAL

5.5.13

The two young Canadian women had come to Seattle solely for the coffee. They'd been in the city for only a day and had already sampled their way through Seattle Coffee Works near Pike Place Market; Espresso Vivace on Broadway; and the veteran Monorail Espresso downtown that had thrived since the early days of Seattle's coffee scene long before Starbucks became a household name. First up on today's morning agenda was a visit to one of Capitol Hill's most renowned coffee roasters, Victrola Coffee on Pike Street.

I was on my way to a Kentucky Derby party, and since Victrola was on my way, I offered to walk my two young visitors from Montreal to their coffee destination.

Walking down Broadway, we talked about Seattle's coffee culture and the ubiquitous Starbucks stores that pepper the town. For a long time, Seattle natives and true coffee aficionados would turn up their noses at any mention of Starbucks. Especially when Howard Schultz stepped down as the company's CEO and their stock was in the can. The world could enjoy their Starbucks, but it was a source of local, bumper-sticker-type pride to buy coffee from an independent shop. You got bonus points if your shop of choice roasted their beans in-house and had an apathetic hipster manning the cash register.

Because these ladies *really* enjoyed their caffeine, and I was curious about their on-the-go lifestyle and how they maintained their energy, our conversation segued into health and healthcare. I explained to them the general anxiety most Americans feel about having no health insurance or insufficient health insurance, and how just one serious illness could bankrupt a person's life savings. They were horrified at the thought of someone losing everything they had worked for because of catastrophic illness or injury.

I believe something intangible and priceless occurs during personal interaction with strangers, when we're no longer just figures in a newspaper or part of a chapter in a textbook. Facts are more viscerally felt when discussing them with a resident of a foreign country rather than simply reading about a current event or a statistic. I was that person to those women.

As we continued our walk, I asked the women if the rumors about long wait times to see a doctor in Canada were true. One of them said that the system is pretty good, overall, but you have to schedule basic, annual checkups about seven months out.

"Because the government pays for it, when it comes to diagnosing an issue, doctors run every test known to man and no stone's left unturned. Sure, we're taxed on everything imaginable (taking up 20–33% of an average to successful person's income) but we use the services, you know?" Because of these frequent, accessible checkups, she said, when her mother got cancer, they found it early, and she is cancer-free today.

And her family didn't go broke because of it.

BOLIVIA

5.7.13

This morning, while it was still quiet, Anna and I chatted at the kitchen table while her handsome boyfriend, Thomas, attended a podiatry convention a couple of miles from the house. I receive a lot of inquiries from conference attendees looking to book rooms, usually for an average of four days. My house is a twenty-five-minute walk or a ten-minute bus ride to the Washington State Convention Center downtown.

Thomas is a practicing podiatrist. Anna is a photographer and trained psychiatrist, but is unable to work in America. Both originally from Bolivia, they now live in San Francisco. Anna would love to be a psychiatrist here, but the thought of getting a work visa and re-establishing her credentials has been too overwhelming, so she has not pursued it. Anna said that practicing in English (she speaks Spanish, Portuguese, Italian, and slightly-accented English), would also be too difficult.

She was interested in my writing work and asked if I got lonely working from home. I told her I enjoyed the peace and quiet, but sometimes missed the old days of working in a bustling real estate office with so many of my friends.

When I was a manager, I had a very large desk and two chairs. Agents and the broker would regularly stop by my desk in the front lobby to talk about their clients, their transactions, and about life in general. With my psychology degree and unquenchable interest in people and their stories, I loved dispensing advice. My agents and I would often joke that I should set up "doctor's hours" and a chaise lounge at my desk. I missed those people profoundly, but I did not miss the stress of the business and the ever-present anxiety of not fulfilling my creative dreams.

Anna seemed dissatisfied with her new life, missing the stimulation and structure of her practice in Bolivia. She'd moved to California to be with Thomas, who'd had been trained as a doctor in America, so his credentials were fine. In fact, his podiatry career was thriving. Since arriving in the United States, Anna had discovered a new hobby, photography, that didn't require credentials and had recently published a book of her photographs.

In the eyes of her friends and family back home, who watched Anna's new life from afar, all seemed well. But she expressed an ongoing frustration, even toward the creative outlet that had given her respite from the misfortune of her abandoned career.

"After I published my book last year, everyone looked at me like, 'Oh, since you've been published, we expect even bigger things from you now.' It has stifled my creativity, and I can no longer pick up a camera because there's so much pressure."

I shamefully admit that while I appeared to be listening to Anna, I was in my own world. I felt envious. I wondered what it must feel like to be published. Reflecting back on the conversation, I suppose I was one more person who was in awe of her seemingly ideal life (one that was clearly by no means perfect).

Anna seemed to be experiencing her life in monochrome discontent, while the world looked on, seeing only vibrant color. As I continue to grow ever more comfortable around strangers, I am constantly reminded that people are almost never what they appear to be at first glance. When Anna walked through my door—young and beautiful, with a handsome doctor boyfriend—all I saw was the story my mind made up about her from this casual observation. But my story was false. Beneath the picture of perfection was a sad woman and discontent artist with a far from perfect life.

She reminded me a lot of myself. Since I'd moved and started my Airbnb venture, I'd also been putting on a false air of confidence for my friends and family. I wanted to look like I had it all together, even though I was riddled with fear about whether my move was a wise decision or if it really was a smart idea to invite strangers into my home.

Funny what we project onto others, while also projecting our own false confidence out into the world. There's a lot of smoke and mirrors going on in our everyday exchanges with people—even those closest to us. As my journey progressed, I was beginning to learn about the value of *not* trying to keep up appearances, and began to consider showing people glimpses of the real me instead.

BELGIUM

They arrived from a place famous for its waffles, but I can't keep them in bagels.

In an effort to give my guests an easy, affordable start to their day of sightseeing or working in Seattle, I offer complimentary breakfast items for them to enjoy. These items are included in the price of their nightly fee. Offerings always include Starbucks VIA instant coffee packets, assorted teas, milk, orange juice, fresh fruit, yogurt, eggs, donut holes, cream cheese, and bagels.

"Do you like bagels?" Marie, my Belgian guest enthusiastically inquired. She had long, brown dreadlocks and a buxom, full figure. Her hippie attire was a natural fit in liberal-minded Seattle, a place known for legalized marijuana use and its acceptance of gay marriage.

"Not really," I casually shrugged. "They're too carb-heavy. Most health-conscious Americans eat them only on rare occasions. There are places like New York, where they're renowned and apparently delicious, but I have never visited there so I can't really say. Many deli shops offer decent varieties—onion, multi-grain, jalapeno, and blueberry. When you order, you can request a gourmet cream cheese schmear, lox, capers, and other toppings."

With eyes as big as saucers at this news, the other Belgian, Camille, dropped her rare "delicacy" in its slot and pressed the special Bagel button on the side of the toaster. Unlike Marie, Camille was slim and blonde and was dressed like an elegant professional. They were a quirky pair, but seemed like a natural fit.

Camille was dying to see what the Bagel button would

do. Having never used it myself, I told her I honestly had no idea.

"Do you think I can pack some bagels in my suitcase and bring them back to Belgium? We don't have them there. We have to travel to Ireland to get bagels." It was my turn to look wide-eyed at Marie. Wow. Who would have known? The things I had been learning about world geography, culture, and culinary nuances continued to entertain me and expand my view of the world.

I assured her that since the grocery store bagels are typically so chock-full of preservatives, they'd probably keep just fine.

Later that night, I made a dedicated trip to the grocery store up the street on Broadway to buy Marie and Camille three types of bagels and three types of cream cheese. Both the fake salmon-flavored cream cheese and the chive spread were a bit of an abomination to my palate. But who am I to judge? I'm the kind of American who occasionally likes to eat Funyuns and pork rinds, so my palate is not that much more sophisticated.

The Belgians are downstairs now, eating a bagel breakfast and packing a bagel lunch, while I'm upstairs, noshing on my egg white omelet and sipping my skinny iced coffee. 'Cause that's how diet-obsessed Americans roll!

* * *

5.10.13

I had coffee with my Bagel Belgians today. We went over some of their recent excursions. I discouraged them from going to the Hoh Rainforest, since they were under the misconception that only took an hour to drive there. The reality is, depending on traffic and ferry lines, the trip can take up to five hours each way.

One of the things I love about this hosting venture is that it's continually refreshing my views on my own city. Every time I have a guest in my home, it offers me a chance to see Seattle through the eyes of a tourist. I've lived in the city since 1989 and though I love it, I sometimes take its charms for granted. I am also fortunate to have developed an extreme familiarity with the city and its surrounding neighborhoods because of my real estate background. This asset has made me a bit of an expert when my visitors are relocating to the city or on a short visit and ask me what they should not miss.

As a longtime resident, it's fun showing my favorite Seattle haunts to visitors and always reminds me why it's such a pleasure to live here. I love Kerry Park and Parsons Garden on Queen Anne; the Kubota Gardens in South Seattle; taking the ferry from the Colman Ferry Dock in downtown and enjoying the half-hour boat ride across the Sound to Bainbridge Island and back; the historic Underground Tour; Pike Place Market on a weekday; the Gum Wall near the Pike Place Market; Smith Tower; the water tower at Volunteer Park near my home; and if you twist my arm—the Space Needle. Go there for a drink, but don't eat there. The views are top-notch, but in a city that's becoming renowned for its culinary scene, the food leaves *a lot* to be desired.

Thus far, Marie and Camille have visited Shilshole Beach, Green Lake, Mt. Rainier, Snoqualmie Falls, and the North Bend outlet mall. Today they're taking Seattle's Underground Tour, visiting the architecturally stunning Downtown Seattle Public Library, and finishing up with a trip to Pike Place Market to pick up provisions for dinner.

These women were serious about their sightseeing. They had really packed it in, and even their plans for the day made my head spin.

"Seattleites are so lucky," Marie said, talking about their recent day trips. "You can drive one hour to ski or hike! Take a public bus for one hour and you're at the beach. All these things would be a twelve-hour drive in Belgium. Your mountains, the lakes, the organic food…" her list trailed off, as if her mind couldn't seem to take in the state's splendor all at once.

"Yep. That's why people move here and never want to leave," I said.

* * *

5.11.13

Last night I was graciously invited to a dinner party…at my own table. I kicked back in a pub chair at the granite countertop and sipped a glass of wine while Marie and Camille efficiently buzzed around my kitchen. They moved comfortably, as if the space were their own.

The greatest thing about my kitchen, according to my guests, is its Viking gas range. I like telling people the story of how, when Jeff and I were dating, we rarely used the stove. Jeff loved taking me out to dinner, and I was happy to let him treat me. Particularly in my days of unemployment, playing the role of starving student.

On the rare occasions he was inclined to cook me dinner, Jeff microwaved cheese sandwiches. I can't justifiably call them grilled cheese sandwiches, because there was no "grilling" to be had. They were expensive, since he made them with Seattle's famous Beecher's Handmade Cheese. He would always look at me expectantly as he placed the gloppy mess in front of me. I didn't have the heart to tell him they were gross and that he was lazy for not using the stove, because he seemed so proud of himself. Guests enjoy my shtick about the cheese sandwiches. It's my attempt to make them feel at ease in the fancy kitchen. I try to assure them that the stove, which cost as much as a used Hyundai, desperately needs to be used.

Marie and Camille also invited over one of their friends, Coen, who lives just down the street. The three have known each other since they were fifteen and are now in their mid-thirties. Coen is the reason for Marie and Camille's visit, as his wife just gave birth to their first child.

While stirring the delicious-looking cream sauce, Marie talked about her lifelong fascination with whales. She told us it's her ultimate wish—number one on her bucket list—to see at least one while visiting the Pacific Northwest. They timed their visit to coincide with the region's whale-watching season, and I was intrigued because it was something I'd never sought out in all my attempts to play tourist in my own town.

"Perhaps it's your spirit animal?" I said.

After some discussion about Native Americans and a person's affinity for a particular identifying animal, Coen mentioned the Belgian Scouts. "But the Scouts are not like they are here in America, where it's all about the cookies," he said, with just a hint of condescension.

He went on to describe how the highly revered Scouts system works in Belgium. A few years after a scout joins the group, and the elders have had time to learn more about a scout's personality, the youth is assigned an animal identifier. Much to Coen's chagrin, his elders assigned him the wombat.

"I had to look up what it was," he said. "Wombats are smart, cushiony, and stubborn. I'm not stubborn," Coen proclaimed, with mock indignation. Apparently "cushiony" was okay with him. Marie and Camille looked at him, smiles in their eyes, shaking their heads knowingly and sipping their glasses of wine in an effort not to contradict him. You could tell the trio was in their element, slipping into familiar roles they'd inhabited for decades.

Camille further explained, "Actually, one of the highest honors is to be assigned the donkey. But, it's rarely bestowed. When you're applying for a job, it's common to mention if you were in the Scouts. Inevitably, the interviewer will ask what your animal was. It's a big thing in Belgium."

Marie laughed and Camille continued, "So, even though being assigned a donkey is a rare honor, you wouldn't put it on your CV, because no one wants to admit that they're an ass."

SOUTH AMERICA

5.11.13

Tonight I came home from the gym and found my new guests, a couple, preparing dinner in the kitchen. I paused, wrestling with a momentary internal debate about whether I should just go up to my room and make dinner out of a box of Triscuits. Even though it was obviously my kitchen, I didn't want to impose on their quiet evening together.

I keep a small refrigerator in my fourth-floor writing loft which makes it possible for me to stow expensive treats and embarrassing food items out of the way of curious guests who share my kitchen fridge. The mini fridge comes in handy when I feel like discreetly slipping up to my room to allow people their privacy.

Both originally from South America, the couple came to the United States for work and had mixed results in their success. The boyfriend now does outreach work in Baja California modernizing Internet connections to that northernmost state in Mexico and other miscellany that he was vague about, or I simply didn't grasp. She lives in Seattle and works as a hostess at a high-end restaurant. After meeting at a wedding through friends of friends, the pair had been dating long distance for a year.

I knew that offering my kitchen as a communal space for guests might be tricky on occasion, but honestly, I wouldn't have it any other way. A traveler myself, when I'm on the road I love taking a break from the expensive (and fattening) restaurant scene. Having a kitchen at one's disposal is an invaluable benefit—for the body and for the wallet—in the home-sharing economy. Each host's level of comfort with people using their common spaces is different, but I like to fully share my house (except my bedroom and rooftop deck) in an attempt to impart a *mi casa es su casa* vibe to my visitors.

The girlfriend perched on the sole pub chair at my kitchen countertop, overseeing her boyfriend's salad-making efforts. Spanish music played softly in the background as I put away my groceries and offered them a bottle of wine to enjoy with their dinner. I apologized for the almost-full dishwasher and moved to make room for their dinner dishes. The boyfriend immediately came to my side, attempting to stop me. "Oh no, please don't worry. I will wash them by hand. I prefer it that way."

A little unsure if he meant it, I confessed to him, "Actually, this is the first time in my adult life that I've had a dishwasher. I prefer to wash them by hand too." Watching us, the young woman smiled and nodded her head in empathetic agreement. Turns out, until recently, she'd never had a dishwasher, either.

"My mom uses her dishwasher to store dirty dishes until she can wash them by hand, and it has always driven me crazy...but now I find myself doing the same thing!" I cried.

"Me too!" exclaimed the girlfriend, pointing at me and laughing boisterously.

Two modern, twenty-first century women, acting like we're still living in a dirt-floor hut.

FRANCE

"When we're not working, we spend a lot of time at work talking about food with our colleagues. Planning meals, talking about what's fresh, and comparing notes on technique. We are obsessed with food—but not in an unhealthy way," said Caroline, my slim Parisian guest.

Simone and Caroline met in engineering school and have been friends for over ten years. Because of the generous French vacation allowances (as much as eight weeks annually), the two women travel together for several weeks a year. Simone lives in Avignon, in the southern part of France, so she and Caroline no longer see one another as much as they did when they went to school and worked together at their first engineering firm. They treasure their annual vacations and have traveled around the world together.

Caroline had only been to the U.S. once before, on a visit to New York City, and Simone had never been to the States, so their excitement, mixed with a little nervousness, was palpable. They chose Seattle because Caroline had been taking English lessons from a language company based out of Seattle. Her engineering firm paid for her language classes and American tutor. After many months of lessons via Skype, the tutor had encouraged Caroline to consider Seattle for her next U.S. visit. Once Simone confirmed she was willing to accompany her, Caroline booked their ten-day stay at my house.

Both women spoke wonderful English, but Caroline's elocution was more polished because of the lessons. Simone was self-conscious of her English-speaking skills and asked me to practice with her and to teach her slang and proper pronunciation. I would purposely pepper our conversations with my awkward French to make her feel less insecure, and we would laugh and laugh about our mutual butchering of one another's native tongue.

Connecting with people in friendship can be like meeting a new love; if you're lucky, the chemistry is magnetic. You just can't help yourself—you want to spend all your time together, and are driven to perform acts of kindness. Simone and Caroline have been unlike any other visitors I have met. From our many days spent together, I've gained insight into French politics, dating, culture, and cooking.

On our Saturday hike up to Poo Poo Point (yes, that's really the name of a mild but exhilarating hike on Tiger Mountain about an hour's drive outside of Seattle), Caroline snapped photos on her fancy SLR camera while Simone enlightened me about the current French president, François Hollande. Many of the French call him "Pudding." According to the women, Pudding's nickname came about because he's physically squishy, politically malleable, and doesn't stand firm on anything. As we trudged up the small mountain, they laughed about their president's physical attributes and shook their heads about his apparent ineptitude. They were passionate about their country and its politics, but neither woman seemed cynical. Humor leavened their frustration.

Days later, while eating dinner at a West Seattle sushi house, I taught Simone and Caroline about online dating and Craiglist.com (they'd never heard of it). Over plates of Emerald City rolls, I convinced them to use my smartphone to check out the online dating offerings in France. We trolled Craigslist in Marseilles and Montpellier, giggling like schoolgirls over posts for men advertising themselves with "clean hands, 40 euro only." It appeared the French Craigslist was more of a prostitution hub than a potential resource for finding a soulmate. By the end of the meal, the women were thoroughly (and justifiably) turned off by the prospect of online dating, but said the meal was some of the best Japanese food they'd ever had.

As a relatively flexible freelancer, my days frequently bend and shape themselves to the offers I receive from guests, often on a whim. When Simone and Caroline expressed interest in whale-watching up in the San Juan Islands, I offered to drive them up to Anacortes to catch the ferry and was pleased when they invited me to join them on their tour.

My offer to drive saved them the cost of renting a car and the hassle of dealing with unfamiliar roads. It also gave me the opportunity to see a scenic part of the Pacific Northwest I'd never visited. I figured it would make me a better host for my future guests if I took the tour.

We enjoyed an amazing day on the boat, spotting three whales and two bald eagles. I left Anacortes with a new awareness about the 172 islands that comprise the spectacular San Juan archipelago. A fact I'd never learned before stepping on the tour boat.

On our way home, knowing the ladies wanted to take souvenirs back to France, I offered to stop at the Seattle Premium Outlets. The outlet mall is a popular stop for tourists and shares a parking lot with the Tulalip Casino, making it an attractive destination for men who want to enjoy themselves while their retail-hungry wives shop. It's located about an hour's drive north of Seattle.

Simone and Caroline were obsessed with Converse shoes and the thought of procuring numerous pairs at a discount made them giddy with delight. As we bee-lined for the Converse store, they chatted about French shoe fashions and how French people abhorred TOMS shoes (calling them walking birth control), but how they adored Converse. Particularly leather Chuck Taylors in black and brown. I laughed at the birth control comment, agreeing that the flat, peasant-style shoes were not the most attractive things. I informed them that the Chuck Taylors fell in and out of fashion with Americans, but seemed to experience a resurgence of interest every decade or so. We cruised every aisle of the Converse store, and I helped them carry piles of boxes as they snapped up shoes for friends and even Caroline's toddler nephew. It was the most exhausting, but fun, day of my hosting career—and it wasn't over yet.

As thanks for my willingness to escort them on this experience-rich day, Simone and Caroline offered to give me a French cooking lesson that night at dinner. Simone's uncle runs a restaurant in Corsica and teaches her all his culinary tricks. The meal was one of the best I've ever eaten—a delicious cod filet with cream sauce, yogurt and beet puree topped with onions and scrambled egg, baked pears stuffed with blue cheese and garlic for the side, and a homemade apple tart for dessert. All the food was paired with French wine, naturally. As the meal progressed, I don't know if I was more intoxicated from the wine or the moment.

I couldn't have been more besotted with Simone and Caroline and our growing friendship. When I was finally able to pry myself from the table, I headed to the Bose SoundDock in the corner of the room and shuffled around for some upbeat music on my iPod. Moving around and working off the decadent, calorie-laden meal seemed like a good idea. Wanting to add even more Seattle flavor to their trip, I put on Macklemore's then-new album and coaxed the ladies into twirling around the living room with me. Simone was smiling ear to ear, her new pink Mariners baseball cap turned backward on her head as she spun me to the energetic sounds of *Can't Hold Us*. We danced for half the album, until the effects of the wine and the late hour finally slowed us down.

Early the next morning, my head pounding from too much wine, I made my way downstairs to enjoy a cup of coffee and share leftover apple tart with Simone and Caroline. As I sipped my coffee, I took an unexpected trip to Toulouse when Simone pulled me in front of her laptop and introduced me virtually to her parents via Skype.

"Bonjour!" I exclaimed, too self-conscious to practice any more of my shoddy French skills. On the screen, I saw the elderly pair, sitting elbow to elbow and smiling broadly with hints of the same smile I'd grown accustomed to seeing grace Simone's face. Simone's dimples matched her mother's and her eyes were the same shade as her father's warm brown ones.

It was the first time her father had ever Skyped, and I was touched that Simone allowed me to share in their moment. I could tell both Simone and her mother were happy he'd finally joined them in connecting on screen. Her father seemed to be nonchalantly taking it in stride, as if it was a technology he'd embraced for years. I could relate. Not to appear like a Luddite, especially compared to the elderly man who had beaten me to the punch, I didn't admit to them that I was also a Skype virgin.

It really is a useful tool, and I'll never forget that memorable first experience. At Simone's request, her mother turned the camera around so I could see their garden and grounds. As her mother walked with her iPad in front of her, Simone pointed out their olive trees, terra cotta terrace, and swimming pool. It had been five years since I'd been to France, and I was surprised by my sudden, visceral urge to feel the warm, scented breeze of an olive grove and to stay in a rustic home steeped with history. In Toulouse, the blue-black sky was tinted with a hint of orange sunset as the day crept toward its end, while I stood in Seattle, drinking coffee in my dining room in my pajamas, hair a mess, exuberantly waving goodbye to her folks on the screen.

Life is unexpected and delightful...and I was sad to drop Simone and Caroline off at the train. We promised each other we'd keep in touch through Skype to continue our mutual butchering of one another's language.

In a world where love affairs, friendships, and professional connections are started and maintained online, I feel fortunate to have met Simone and Caroline through the Internet. Airbnb brought us together and offered me friendships I didn't even know I needed, but now can't imagine my life without.

All around us, digital stories spread like wildfire to inspire the chronically lonely and single. My Airbnb friendships are an inspiration to me, and I don't want to go back to what my life was like before them. I'm in awe that this cutting-edge, sharing way of life has been embraced by society, and I am humbled to be a part of it. In addition to offering a service to travelers, this virtual platform has allowed people to forge bonds that are real, tangible...and I hope, long-lasting.

LAUNDRY DAY

6.9.13

News from the house this week? A high turnover of guests…and a broken dryer.

I haven't had to visit a Laundromat for over fifteen years. And even when I did, I went not out of necessity but merely to accompany a boyfriend so he wouldn't be bored. I have been fortunate to have had an in-house washer and dryer wherever I've lived. This is pretty common in the Northwest.

Admittedly, there is a part of me that has forever romanticized the Laundromat. In my daydreams I think, *"Look at all those movie meet-cutes where the girl leaves a granny panty in the dryer and it gets returned by the hunky guy who goes to use the machine right after her! After finding the cotton talisman—an equivalent of the dropped handkerchief of the '50s—the man walks confidently toward the girl with her panty hooked in the crook of his index finger and a wry grin on his face. All this, before he effortlessly and confidently asks her out!"* Um, yeah. This is Seattle. Reality is more nuanced than the meet-cute movie version.

The downside of using the Laundromat in my neighborhood so close to downtown? Crackheads—lots o' crackheads. Yesterday, while my dryer did its sixteen minutes of magic, I watched a woman walk around rambling incoherently to herself, wearing a tie-at-the-neck halter top…around her ass. Perhaps she was washing a more suitable outfit?

The upside? This innkeeper can wash and dry two queen sheet sets, four bath towels, four washcloths, and two hand towels—*in less than an hour*—for only eight bucks. Plus,

Laundromats have bountiful vending machines that taunt you into spending your spare quarters. Eating some Red Vines and watching the *Crackhead Follies* live is often better than most movies at the local multiplex. Really. Even if you're not an innkeeper, if it's convenient for you to do so, I heartily endorse a trip to the Laundromat the next time your schedule won't allow for several hours' worth of clothes washing.

Busy times are a consideration. As a freelancer, it's easy for me to go in the middle of the day when it's quiet, but expect more competition for machines if you work a regular schedule and need to go during prime time. I suspect my heady appreciation for the Laundromat comes from a naïveté due to my middle of the week, daytime visits. I know all you weekend Laundromat visitors who have to go out of necessity are likely rolling your eyes right now.

If you're considering hosting, make sure you have lots of sturdy sheet sets and towels on hand to save you hours of laundry. IKEA makes inexpensive sheet sets in vibrant prints that photograph well. But you'll trade a lot of softness for their steel-like durability.

I buy most of my sheet sets on sale at Macy's, or at Ross, Target, and Marshalls. All of these retailers also sell great, durable towels. Another tiny consideration? Stock up on microfiber bath mats; they're really easy to wash and dry and mine have held up admirably for an entire year. Or consider towel-style bath mats. Don't use the same bath rug between guests—that's just nasty. Again, stray pubic hairs—especially foreign ones—are *never* welcome!

Macy's always seems to have a great sale going on, and they have easy financing plans for buying mattresses. There's nothing like dropping cash on two mattress sets at once to give you a case of sticker shock, trust me. Even if you're only buying one, buy it new and write that puppy off on your business expenses. Due to the recent surge in bedbugs, don't buy a used mattress unless you really know the person who's selling it. Also, assume that your guests have likely traveled around a bit before arriving on your doorstep, and invest in bedbug protector mattress covers. I also recommend pillow covers and an additional mattress cover. This upfront expense is a lot cheaper than hiring an exterminator or suffering even one review from a guest that discovers an issue before you do. No one wants to sleep with bedbugs. A review like that would effectively suspend your listing and turn away potential guests for the foreseeable future.

Also, you can bet there's going to be a lot of action happening in *and on* your guest bed, so plan your extra duvet covers, blankets, and decorative pillows accordingly.

QATAR

6.13.13

Lodging in the ground-floor room this week is a man from Milan who owns an apparel company. He's here on business, deciding whether to base his U.S. operations out of Seattle or Los Angeles.

Working in the garment industry is quite a change of pace for him after the last four years he's spent in Qatar, working with FIFA to bring the highly-coveted World Cup Games to the Arab state. Offering me a little insight into the country, he explained that much like Russia and China's rigorous Olympic training camps of the '80s, the Qatari are plucking young kids from Africa and South America and bringing them to Qatar to train to be elite athletes.

Since native Qataris are quite small in stature, the country's soccer enthusiasts decided to construct a new breed of "native" player. What the Qatari lack in stature, they make up for in healthy coffers. Youths are enticed to abandon their families and the slums of their homelands to move to opulent Qatar for education, a Qatari passport, and the possibility of future fame. For those who like to place bets, make note of the Qatari soccer team in the next six or so years. These relocations are a calculated attempt to create well-honed soccer machines who'll wear Qatari jerseys when the country hosts the World Cup in 2022.

My guest describes the Qatari as loving their massive SUVs and having a penchant for alcohol. While driving in Qatar, he said he often felt that death on the road was imminent—not from Qatari military personnel or some random threat, but from the Hummer idling next to him, inevitably being driven by a woman clad in a burqa and dark Ray-Bans. With their vision impaired by the burqa and the sheer size of the vehicle—many women could barely see over the dash. They often veered into his lane, or he'd regularly see accidents littering the roads, the scenarios familiar. Petite women, standing outside their gigantic vehicles, screaming into their cellphones and gesturing wildly with their hands.

"As an Islamic state," the man continued, "alcohol cannot be sold to native residents of Qatar. But it is legal to sell liquor and beer to expats and temporary workers. This creates a raging black market for the juice—and a lot of fast 'friends' for a newly arrived worker."

The one caveat on the sale of alcohol? Visitors may only spend 10% of their salary on booze. So what does a temporary worker and non-native do? He goes to his company's HR department and asks for a letter that states a highly exaggerated salary. Letter in hand, he drives to the nearest liquor store (of which there are few), spends wildly and stuffs his trunk with booze to sell to all his new friends.

"But wait!" my guest exclaimed. "You can't drive around with liquor in your car—it's against Qatari law!" Bribes flow as readily as the $15 bottles of beer sold at the hotels. Black market booze is the new Wild West on this Persian Gulf peninsula.

If this sounds attractive, be prepared for 120-degree temperatures. Because it's the heart of the opulent Middle East, you're probably going to need some fashionable new clothes. Luckily, I have a new Italian connection and can hook you up on where to buy some couture designs.

SOUTH KOREA

6.21.13

It may not surprise you to hear that in addition to my habit of people-pleasing, I am also not so good with boundaries.

Staying in the house this past week? An entire Korean family...in one small room. The night they arrived, the father asked if their grown son (who was graduating from the University of Washington later that week) could also stay in their room. I presumed it would be a one-time thing. Like maybe they'd had an exhausting travel day and didn't want to drive him home in their rental car to wherever he lived. Judging by the son's 253 area code, I guessed that he lived down in Tacoma—about an hour south of Seattle by car. Or, perhaps now that school was out for the summer, maybe he'd been kicked out of his old dorm? I wasn't sure what was going on, but I told the father that the son staying over would be fine.

One night turned into seven, and the whole family slept in my third-floor bedroom the entire duration of their stay. The room has only a queen bed and a generous walk-in closet, so I guess the young man either shared the bed with his parents or made a bed for himself on the floor—or in the closet. In addition to the fact that their son lodged with them for free, they also had received the benefit of a reduced rate, because they booked at my weekly rate of seven nights for the price of six.

When Annie initially counseled me on tips for hosting, she advised me to offer discount weekly and monthly rates. Monthly rates are four weeks for the price of three (whatever my nightly rate is at the time, multiplied by 21).

Weekly rates are seven nights for the price of six. It was very common in those first months to get week-long visitors, but I nixed the weekly rate as the summer months and high season approached. It simply wasn't necessary, given my sweet location and growing list of online reviews.

I didn't have the heart to tell the father I would have charged them more money for an extra guest if I'd known the son would be there the entire week—showering *twice* a day. Even if I had the confidence to charge him for the extra guest, I was unsure of what a fair surcharge would be. Ten dollars? Perhaps fifteen? The situation was new territory for me. The only people who'd inquired about children staying in the room were parents traveling with young toddlers. I was totally unprepared for a grown child's unexpected stay.

One night in the living room, feeling tipsy and generous after conversing with the Korean family and sharing drinks with the man from Milan, I stealthily slipped a clean bath towel for their son into the Koreans' bedroom. I worried about him—I imagined him drying off with washcloths for his two showers a day—though I had no idea if he was actually doing this. Again with the people-pleasing. It's how I'm wired.

The evening of Operation Towel Drop, I learned about the son's required two-year stint in the Korean Navy after high school, and how he had hated every minute of it. I wasn't aware that in South Korea, they have three branches of military, similar to our four. They have a navy, air force, and army.

I also learned from talking to them that evening exactly what this family of South Koreans thought of North Koreans. "They're scrawny, like little birds," said the son. "You can tell they're from the north by their tiny little heads," he said, somewhat disdainfully, while cupping his hands in front of him, suggesting something roughly the size of a baseball. The family was vehemently opposed to the actions of their northern neighbors and cringed at any suggestion of association to the shenanigans of the "other Korea."

I noticed, with a hint of irony, that boundaries were very important to this family. If only my personal boundaries were as firm as the boundary in their patriotic hearts that separated them from their northern neighbors.

The next morning, when I came downstairs to make coffee, I immediately felt better about my lack of assertiveness. Groggily looking to my left as I reached the base of the stairs, I saw the mother and son sitting on the floor in front of the fireplace. Ink black hair illuminated by the glow of the fire in the unlit room, their heads were bent together in whispered conversation.

I didn't know what they were saying, but to an outside observer, it was clear something precious was taking place. A mother, who hadn't seen her only child in years, was enjoying the opportunity to sip a cup of tea and to catch up with her boy without distractions. With the father absent, their dynamic together had softened and appeared less formal than it was when he was around. Saying nothing, I turned away to make my coffee at the stove. I now realized the conversations I *should* have had about an extra guest in that small room would have made me feel cheap as I witnessed that tender moment.

The morning they left, the parents walked around my house with a camera, snapping photos of my art and common spaces. Handing me the tiny digital camera, the mother asked me first to take a picture of the family, then swap places with the son so she would have a photograph with me and her husband. She wanted to show their friends back home what I looked like. Somewhere in South Korea, there's a picture of me with mussed hair, wearing glasses and a blue T-shirt, standing with my arms around the sweet couple.

As she turned to go upstairs to pack their bags, the mother bowed her hands forward and gingerly offered me a decorative cord with the beaded mahogany faces of Tragedy and Comedy carved at the top. It was a kind, unexpected gift, and yet another confirmation to me that I did the right thing by not having an awkward conversation about the son's unexpected stay. The gift was obviously something she'd brought from Korea, intending to gift it to their American host even before she'd met me. I was touched by her thoughtfulness and the uniqueness of the gift, which reminded me of my days spent in Asia as a child.

The cord hangs from the doorknob of my office and will forever remind me of the juxtaposition of assertiveness and inaction and what *not* having boundaries with that family turned out to be worth.

DENVER & RENO

6.23.13

My introduction to today's ground-floor guests came via my cell phone. I was at a chic, private event for a friend's birthday party at Oola, a new distillery with an event space in Capitol Hill. Happily sipping my third cocktail and talking with a cute guy, I missed the vibration in my pocket from their first call. I didn't hear the second call, either—it must have been drowned out by the DJ's thumping electronic music. Eventually, I excused myself from conversation with the chatty man and noticed that I'd missed two calls. I knew that calls from unfamiliar area codes usually meant a guest was trying to reach me. With some trepidation, I stepped outside where it was quieter to listen to the message.

Only two and a half months into my new venture, my worst nightmare as a host had come true. In the voice mail, Jackie introduced herself and informed me that the toilet in her bathroom was not flushing. Friends, especially my male friends, know I am fairly, ahem, "remedial" when it comes to fixing a toilet. Even though I spent years managing an office and regularly playing plumber when the company bathrooms backed up, I loathe using a plunger and like to use my "girl card" to have men fix backed up toilets for me. Don't judge! Toilets are not my friends.

I called Jackie back and told her I would be home within thirty minutes. I apologized to the birthday girl and slipped out of her party to slog the twenty blocks home in the pouring rain (in heels). As I walked, I called Dave, a guy friend who's a firefighter and home inspector. I warned him he might be fielding my desperate SOS call later if I couldn't figure out what was wrong with the toilet. Because he was on a shift at the firehouse that night, he couldn't help me, but assured me he'd offer phone support and walk me through the repair process, if needed.

Every bedroom in my house has its own full bathroom. Which is a great selling feature in my ads, but means there's no general bathroom for people to use in the common areas. This can be tricky when I have friends over to hang out. I ask them not to use my guests' bathrooms and make them go upstairs to use the bathroom in my third-floor bedroom.

As I teetered home, feet aching and hands clutching my umbrella, I silently prayed I'd sober up by the time I reached home. Gingerly dodging puddles, my thoughts ran wild with visions of my guests creeping up two flights of stairs in the middle of the night to use my toilet if I couldn't get theirs to work. Not fun for anyone, and the thought of it was powerful incentive to kick off my heels, put on my big girl plumber pants, and figure out how to fix the problem.

Coming into the foyer, I cautiously looked into the bedroom situated only six feet from the front door. Inside, I saw an older woman with short, spiked hair lounging at the head of the bed in her pink bathrobe. She was propped up on a pillow, reading on her iPad. I tapped a gentle warning on the bedroom door and poked my head in. Jackie again introduced herself, saying she was from Reno, as I shook hands with her sister, Julie, who was from Denver. Since hanging up the phone with me, Jackie had once again tried to plunge the toilet, to no avail.

After some initial small talk (which, admittedly, also bought me some time to sober up), I rolled up my sleeves and tried my hand at defeating my nemesis. I was determined not to let the toilet win. After a few deep thrusts of the plunger and some loud gurgles—and an appreciative audience cheering me on from the bed—a purple condom appeared. What a lovely way to further kill my cocktail buzz. Though I was completely grossed out, I was relieved and glad that I was the one who found this thoughtful souvenir from a former guest, and not the pair of sisters, who were too far in bedroom to see my discovery.

Stealthily depositing this "treasure" in the wastebasket with the plunger and hiding it with some discarded Kleenex on top, I told them it must have been a fluke clog and wished them good night. If I could greet my guests and unclog a toilet barely sober, I felt like I could now overcome any obstacle my new business threw my way.

* * *

The next morning I came downstairs to make coffee and chat with Jackie and Julie. I'd apparently won their admiration after averting the toilet crisis the night before.

They booked my place for two nights, planning to see Seattle before leaving on an Alaskan cruise with several members of their family. If you're considering hosting, two-night minimums are another thing I strongly suggest. In an effort not to run you or your cleaning person into the ground, factor in the hour or so it takes to clean each room and to do the laundry for a one-night stay. Do you want to be doing that several times a week? Decide if it's worth it to you and set your minimum-stay requirement accordingly. I have a caveat at the bottom of both my listings that says if a guest is willing to pay a higher cleaning rate, I'll consider a one-night stay. However, no one has ever asked to stay for just one night, and the Airbnb platform doesn't make it easy to change your minimum-night setting back and forth.

I stirred cream into my coffee and listened sympathetically as the ladies relayed news that their plans for the family cruise had grown complicated. Jackie's daughter had just called to inform the sisters that their 86-year-old, nearly blind mother had fallen and broken her foot three hours after the women had left their respective homes to fly to Seattle. This would be unfortunate news on any day, but the terrible timing of this accident threatened to affect the entire family's plans. Their mother was slated to fly to Seattle with Jackie's daughter the morning of their cruise to join them on their Alaska adventure. Jackie was her mother's full-time caregiver. Both sisters were understandably concerned about their mother's health and worried she wouldn't make her flight or the cruise. But they were also bummed out that their long-awaited vacation was on the verge of being cancelled altogether. Who wouldn't be?

It had become an annual family tradition that their mother would take the two sisters, their brother, and all their grown children on exotic trips to far-flung destinations. They'd visited Asia, Australia, Mexico, Hawaii, and recreational hotspots like Disneyland and Disney World in America. But in recent years, these family trips had been a little more difficult, because their mother had become prone to bouts of low blood sugar, which occasionally caused her to collapse.

This happened one year when the family was on a cruise through the British Isles. While heading to the dining hall on the massive ship one evening, their mom had fallen in an elevator. The cruise company, fearing further medical complications, sent nine crew members up to their stateroom to pack their belongings. They had the entire family packed in under an hour, and the ship unceremoniously deposited them in the nearest port. The sisters recall walking to a waterfront hotel and inquiring as to what town they were in, keenly aware that they wore the costume of Stupid American admirably.

Despite their abandonment in port, the ladies said they ended up having a great time befriending the locals and enjoying the town pubs. Plus, they left the United Kingdom armed with a great travel story to tell for years to come.

If their mother was unable to make this trip to Alaska, they said, it probably signaled the end of a lifetime of travel for her—and for them as a family. It sounded like the mother, and her pocketbook, was the glue that had kept the family together on all the trips. As they said the words, it seemed particularly gut-wrenching for Jackie and Julie to discuss this weighty reality aloud versus keeping their worst fear cloaked in self-contained anxiety or false optimism.

Later that day, I came downstairs to leave the house and stopped to chat in the doorway of their room. They were in comfortable lounging clothes, nestled comfortably side by side in the way that only close sisters and best friends who've spent hours curled up in bed chatting together can.

Noting my workout clothes, they asked where I was going (which should have been obvious, but in casual Seattle, you never know). I told them I was off to Pilates class and was valiantly attempting to reestablish a workout habit and lose the ten-pound beer weight that clung to my petite frame. I felt it was criminal not to take advantage of all the gyms, yoga studios, and Pilates classes at my disposal in my new neighborhood.

Julie, the quiet sister, lamented that the Pilates studio in her neighborhood had just closed. In my sometimes snobbish, cosmopolitan mind, I had an instant visual of the gray strip malls studded with Subway sandwich shops and David's Bridal boutiques that probably surrounded Julie's plain-vanilla suburban neighborhood in Denver. Who doesn't like Pilates? I bet they didn't have many Whole Foods or yoga studios either!

Jackie told me to keep up the good work on maintaining my figure because eventually it would go to hell in a handbasket. This type of unsolicited advice is frequently doled out by older women everywhere to their younger, firmer counterparts, with the younger person invariably refusing to believe their fate will be similar to that of the admonisher. We all want to believe we won't become like our elders, like somehow, against the odds, our paths will be different.

I studied the two sisters in the bed, wondering if I'd someday be like them. I think that's what frightens many of us most of all about strangers. Especially poor people, older people, and people who are heavier than we are. We search out our similarities and differences, and often our worst fears play out when we get a glimpse of what could be our future by seeing folks as they are now. So many of our actions with one another are laced with the nuances of poignant memories and future fears. As I stood before them, it was clear their advice was rooted in the past and their long-ago youth.

"When I was your age, I weighed 107 pounds, ate whatever I wanted, never worked out, and had a figure like an hourglass. Now look at me," Jackie said, looking down at her breasts resting happily on her biceps, her robe covering a torso that had become more stopwatch than hourglass. "One day you look in the mirror and say, 'Oh shit. Mom?'"

It was a poignant statement out of the mouth of a woman bravely facing her mother's newly incapacitated state and what it meant for them both. Despite our worst fears about aging or our attempts to slow down the hands of time, that hourglass will eventually have its way with all of us.

SUMMER

The last week of April, I noticed a flurry of emails arriving from college students around the country wanting to book two- and three-month summer stays in my home. I soon discovered that all the big businesses in town sent out their intern acceptance letters that week and gave students notice of their summer pay and lodging allowances. By month's end, I was receiving an average of three messages a day from students hoping to be my roommate for the summer.

Since I was still inexperienced in the world of hosting, and only had Annie's peer advice to go on, it hadn't occurred to me that people might want to stay with me for months at a time. It felt too good to be true to realize I would be able to book two interns (at a very lucrative monthly rate for each room) and have my summer free to enjoy like a normal person.

When I signed up for the Airbnb gig, I envisioned my weekends being dominated by an endless cycle of laundry, cleaning, and greeting new guests. A part of me feared my new lifestyle would separate me from my cohorts who were off enjoying brunches, weekends out of town, and a more carefree existence. To a large extent, my new life tethered me to my home and made me feel separate from other people because of its unique demands. Beyond telling friends I couldn't accompany them for weekend hikes because I had a room (or rooms) to clean, I worried about how my unique situation would affect my romantic life when I decided to start dating again. Would I ever be able to stay over at his place or take an unexpected romantic getaway out of town?

Not every host has to commit to this kind of non-stop

schedule. Airbnb's calendar system allows you to block off days and weeks according to the demands of your schedule and personal life. Perhaps you're a person who merely wants to open up a room on the weekends, or even just one weekend a month to make a little extra money. Some people only list their space when they are away traveling. That's okay! The model allows you to open your doors as much or as little as you feel comfortable.

In my case, to stay afloat financially as I continued to advance in my freelance career and build my client list, I needed to keep the house as full as possible and was determined to put in whatever effort was necessary to make it work. Even at the expense of my romantic life. The eventual confirmation of two long-term summer interns was an unexpected gift of a normal life, allowing me to feel more like my friends, and it also really lightened my workload. It was nice to look forward to fewer daily emails from would-be guests, and not as many cleaning and laundry demands.

One of the two interns, Alison, actually brought her boyfriend Alistair along, so I had three people in the house with me from late June to late August. Within a week of their arrival, after I was sure they were all settled, I used air miles to escape to California to visit my friend Hilary and enjoy a vacation of my own.

I think it's wonderful that so many people have romantic notions of retiring and running a traditional bed and breakfast. (Cue the mental image of a two-story gingerbread house on Cape Cod.) While I now know firsthand that it can be endlessly fascinating to meet guests from around the world, the thought of spending my golden years rushing to keep up on laundry, cleaning, bookkeeping, cooking, and entertaining sounds exhausting. What I appreciate about the Airbnb model is it allows people like me—a working professional with a lot of extra room to spare—the chance to host people and to make money for retirement *while* I am still young.

After explaining to people what Airbnb is and telling them I'm a host, one of the top five questions I get is, "Do you have to cook breakfast for guests?" No. No, I do not.

The listings on the site do not generally resemble a typical bed and breakfast, though as more traditional places catch on to the model, there will likely be a lot more listings that do. In many ways, my house feels like a bed and breakfast, sans frilly bed skirts and antique décor. But you will never find me down in the kitchen in my apron, cooking you eggs. I wouldn't torture you like that. I trust if I leave 'em in the fridge for you and tell you to help yourself, you'll likely do a better job cooking them than I could.

I've seen many hosts on the site who like to cook for their guests, though it's not expected. And to them, I say, "Good on ya!" Offering this benefit is entirely optional and depends on your culinary inclinations. I am sure if your schedule allowed you to make breakfast for your guests every morning, you could command a higher nightly rate and cater to clientele who desire those services.

An added benefit I extended to my long-term intern guests was access to my washer and dryer so they could manage their own laundry. This is a courtesy I offer to all guests who stay longer than four days. As someone who has traveled for weeks at a time, I'd never want to make my guests have to go in search of the Laundromat, or to spend valuable vacation time waiting for their laundry to finish.

I also offered the interns extra sheets and towels, but how often they chose to wash and change their linens was up to them. As the summer progressed, I grew more relaxed in my innkeeper role and was getting better at reeling in my hyper-mothering and people-pleasing tendencies. I was happy to release the reins and let my summer roommates live comfortably in the house, while I was out of sight traveling and working on writing projects.

ALI & ALI

"We know we want to incorporate Persian, Chinese, and American influences into our wedding. We call ourselves 'traditional,' but beyond that, we don't know what other adjectives to use to describe what we want. We both love watermelon. Do you think we could somehow incorporate that?"

I felt like I was on one of my floral consultations from the year before I started my Airbnb venture. But I was actually sitting comfortably in my dining room working on flower recipes. (Much like the culinary world, floral designers plot out the "ingredients" that make up their bouquets and arrangements. Eight roses, six tulips, five ranunculus, and so on as they coordinate each specific design.) After noting the numerous buckets of flowers I had purchased to do flower arrangements and bouquets for a friend's weekend wedding—filling the entire living room, they were impossible to miss—and learning some details about my former design life, Alison and Alistair had a lot of questions for me.

"What tends to be the most expensive flower? How much do bouquets cost? Why do wedding flowers cost so much?" I fielded one question at a time, and explained the concept of overhead, international floral auctions, and other nuances of the flower world—like the fact that carnations cost more than a rose, but are less valued—and I could tell Alison and Alistair were fascinated. "We should be taking notes," she said.

I couldn't help glancing down at Alison's bare left ring finger—that I was pretty sure had been bare all summer. They'd been living with me since late June. When booked their two-month stay during her summer internship at a real estate company downtown, Alison said her boyfriend of four years would be accompanying her to Seattle. Seeing her naked finger, I was dying to ask if a summer proposal had taken place that they hadn't yet mentioned.

But with them, I could tell; the fact they'd one day marry was simply a given. Over the weeks of observing them around the house, I'd noted the gentle and respectful ways they talked to one another. How they loved spending evenings together, heads bent reading a book on the couch or focused on a board game at the coffee table. They acted like they were still in the honeymoon phase of their courtship, even though they'd long ago surpassed that eighteen-month mark.

Alistair was a temporarily laid-off contract worker who didn't have to report back to his tech job until they returned home to Minnesota, so he spent a lot of time in the townhouse during the day. While I was working upstairs, I'd regularly catch whiffs of delicious smells emanating from the kitchen. I'd often wander down from my writing loft and find him experimenting with ingredients he'd bought at Pike Place Market. Alistair loved buying exotic vegetables that he'd never seen back home and had no idea what to do with. Things like okra, black radishes, and jicama. When Alison came in from work in the evenings, he'd typically have dinner waiting for her. His care of her and kind actions toward me during our shared days in the townhouse reaffirmed what a wonderful husband Alistair would be to Alison. They frequently invited me to share in whatever delicacy he'd concocted that day. But in an effort to give them privacy and allow them to retain some sense of their normal life back in Minneapolis, I often declined.

That August day at the table, as I was arranging my friend's bridal bouquet, I realized how few times we'd actually sat down at the dinner table together. Their stay with me was nearly over. As they watched me pruning stems and contemplating ribbon colors, they reminisced about good and bad weddings they'd attended all over the country in the past year. They'd attended rustic do-it-yourself weddings and opulent weddings at four-star hotels. As if on cue, they told me it seemed like all of their late-twentysomething friends were suddenly getting married.

As I worked, I listened to their stories and naturally settled into my usual conversational role as bridal consultant. It was effortless to rehash tips I'd learned from my most recent stint working in the wedding industry. "Start collecting pins on Pinterest now, so you can one day help your vendors understand your aesthetic. And if you can afford it, hire a planner. Or at minimum, a 'day-of' coordinator. Your friends and family are there to enjoy your wedding, not schlep chairs around and worry about when the baker's going to show up with the cake. Spend your money on a good photographer; never skimp on that decision, as you're going to look at those memories for the rest of your life, and you'll want them to be great. Secure your venue first, your photographer second, and your florist third." I was surprised by how quickly and easily these tips rolled off my tongue.

I had dabbled on and off in the floral world since I was eighteen years old, and I still occasionally miss it. I loved interacting with brides in the early stages of their planning and, ultimately seeing them all dolled up on their wedding day. Once, when a setup went overly long at the reception area that housed the doorway leading to the ceremony aisle, I stood silently with my fellow floral workers as the bride and her father shared a sweet moment before stepping out in front of their guests. The man leaned in to his daughter and said quietly, but still loud enough for us to hear from five feet away, "Bree, this is the proudest day of my life." Even today, the memory of that scene still brings tears to my eyes.

Being able to witness intimate moments like the one Bree and her father shared almost made earning barely above minimum wage worthwhile. But the difficult brides who demanded perfection on their wedding days were too hard for me to stomach. I'll never be the girl who worries about rain on her wedding day or if her bridesmaids' shoes all match. It was wonderful to have a creative outlet, but it was hard to work with stressed-out women who struggled over every minor decision as if those inconsequential details were more important than the marriage itself. Eventually the job became way too much of a headache to manage doing even part-time, so I went back to doing weddings only when it seemed like fun and as favors for friends.

Somewhere along the way in my conversation with Alison and Alistair, we turned from talking about adjectives that describe weddings to adjectives that describe home. As they looked around the house we'd been amicably sharing all summer, they asked me to describe my aesthetic.

I am a fan of the wabi-sabi aesthetic, which sees beauty in imperfection, and I want my home to reflect this sense of forgiving accessibility. If my décor is presented as less than perfect, my hope is people will feel at home and free to do things like put their feet up on the coffee table and use the good crystal.

When guests compliment me on my décor, I regale

them with well-worn stories about the thrift stores and antique shops where I found my inexpensive, quirky treasures. Things like the gold tractor nestled on a Blitz-Weinhard's beer can—a trophy that Grayson's dad won from a tractor derby in the '80s and I begged Grayson for in the breakup; the "R" from a retired Starbucks sign that Grayson and I found at an antique store in Centralia, Washington, on a road trip back from Oregon wine country; and the $20 Italian mandolin I bought at a yard sale from a woman whose grandmother purchased it at an auction in the 1940s. I think my dented, but beautiful things offer insight into who I am as a person. I believe our houses and their décor tell stories about us, and our interior spaces reflect our interior lives.

I asked Alison and Alistair to describe their home back in the Midwest. Alistair talked about the house's three stories and prime location on a corner lot. In a quirky twist in their unfolding narrative as a couple, the reality show *House Hunters* had followed them for five days as they shopped for a house. Their realtor was thrilled that HGTV was filming their search—any realtor knows that a half-hour long television show is impressive (and free!) advertising for their business.

Coincidentally, in late July while walking down a street near my place, Alison and Alistair heard repeated honking and their names being called. Since they knew no one in the area, they both considered it a fluke and kept walking, confident that whoever it was, wasn't addressing them. The honking continued as they walked, until they eventually turned and saw their Minneapolis realtor. He was passing by in a bright white rental car, wearing a handsome tuxedo and a huge grin. His wife had angled her body over his in the driver's seat and was boisterously waving at Alison and Alistair—no doubt thrilled to be making a small-world connection so far from home. Apropos to our conversation, the realtor and his wife were visiting Seattle for a wedding.

As I educated Alison and Alistair about weddings and we volleyed stories back and forth about home and our mutual love of thrift shops—I realized I was learning things too. When I pictured them in their new home, slowly filling it with all the treasures that really defined it as "theirs" as a couple, I found myself wistfully thinking of my own romantic future.

I want the guy who's gonna help me lug home that free, wooden coffee table we find propped up next to a Dumpster, and share my thrill in finding it. I want the emotionally available man who's going to sit next to me at the table on a sunny Saturday afternoon, imagining aloud the details of our future wedding as if it's the most natural thing in the world, even if I don't yet have that engagement ring on my finger. When I looked at the sweet couple, I was filled with hope—for them and for myself.

Through good conversation, we often learn we want something we didn't yet know we needed. My world continues to change as I step, with strangers, to the easy rhythm of histories shared. Each time I sit down to really engage with a guest, I'm offered insight into their lives, and my viewpoints on life evolve and grow. I am in the rare position to have renewable opportunities to talk about myself and to learn from a revolving door of strangers—a priceless dynamic that I feel fortunate to have stumbled upon.

Because I *had* stumbled and was in the process of picking myself back up, it was even more meaningful to have the opportunity to create a different life for myself, with a different world view.

NICOLA

My second summer guest was Nicola, a Mormon woman from Idaho hired for a two-month intern gig at an accounting firm. Prior to her booking the ground-floor "Garden Room," she told me she liked to cook and work in the yard. I figured with her stated green thumb, she'd be a natural fit for the room. Perhaps the modest yard space would offer her a welcome reprieve from her long hours at the office. I had a fleeting vision of her creating raised vegetable beds and tending to my diseased Japanese maple tree.

Nicola showed up in a black town car on a warm evening in late June. Her employer, an esteemed Fortune 500 company, had offered her a generous allowance for lodging and extras—like car services to take her to and from the airport. I helped Nicola with her bags and got her situated in her room. Hoping to acquaint her with her new surroundings, I offered to take her on a walking tour of Capitol Hill.

Nicola was a tad overweight, so I had to slow my pace to facilitate her comfort, which didn't bother me at all. I wanted to allow her time to take in all the new scenery and to get a sense of her new neighborhood. Whenever I meet a new guest, I try to think about how I would like to be treated if I were in their position. Because I have been treated with kindness and saint-like patience by locals when I've been the bumbling stranger in a foreign land, I try to remember this when I am showing someone around town. I consider it good travel karma and payback for all the generous people I have been fortunate to encounter in my life.

As we walked past the local cinema, Nicola breathlessly mentioned a love of film and said she'd worked in a video store back in the days of VHS tapes.

Her comment reminded me that she was not the typical college intern. Nicola was in her mid-thirties, around my age, and had transitioned to college and Mormonism after growing up in South America with very little schooling or religious upbringing. She told me she had a married sister on the East Coast and a mother who still lived in Uruguay. Nicola mentioned this because she hoped one or both of them might visit her at some point during the summer, and hoped that would be okay.

I always allow guests to bring visitors into my home as long as they ask permission first. Naturally, there's the possibility—rarely discussed—that one of my single guests might get lucky and pick up a one-night stand, but I don't get too worked up at the thought. As far as I know, it hasn't happened yet, and I've never encountered an unexpected stranger in my house.

Airbnb allows hosts an opportunity to list their "House Rules" on the site, and I ask only a handful of things from my guests: 1) Take shoes off at the door, as the carpets and hardwoods are new. 2) Observe quiet time after 11:00 p.m. out of respect for the other guests and neighbors. 3) Clean up after yourself. 4) Turn off lights and appliances after use. 5) Practice the Golden Rule. These rules are pretty simple, and so far I have had only minor, forgettable issues.

After Nicola and I finished our tour of the neighborhood and were headed back home, she asked if we could stop at the grocery store to pick up a few items for her workday lunches. From what little Nicola had told me, and knowing she was an accountant, I assumed the woman was fiscally prudent and great at managing her pennies. I considered it a nod of approval to the monthly pricing of my rooms that she'd chosen my place above others and mentally patted myself on the back.

Returning to the townhouse, Nicola unpacked her groceries and staked out real estate in the kitchen cupboards. I began the creative shuffle of making space for four adults in the compact kitchen we would all share for the next two months. My kitchen is beautiful but severely lacking in cupboard space.

It's occurred to me that a lot of what draws me to Airbnb is learning the delicate dance of negotiating personal space with others. Having lived alone most of my adult life, sharing space with people I could not influence and cajole (like I did growing up with my family) did not come naturally to me. I was, embarrassingly, not very good at it. Perfectionists, like me, keep a clean space, but don't make for the best roommates if they're sharing space with folks who are not Type A. I've only lived with lazy men, and therefore never relished the thought of long-term roommates. But I was striving to grow and let go of some of my past rigidity. Baby steps.

What is perfect about Airbnb? Its ephemeral and transient nature. Your "roommates" leave after a few days, or stay, at most, for a few months. Plus, you never have to harass them to pay rent or chip in their share of the utility bills. Hosts can put a cap on the highest number of days in a row they're willing to allow guests to stay. I have set my cap at a generous 180 days, but the site allows up to 365 nights. I haven't taken the plunge to up my cap to 365 days, as the thought of it seems like way too much of a commitment and defeats the purpose of what attracts me to Airbnb—meeting lots of new people.

Given the different personalities that abound in this

world, and everyone's varying level of cleanliness expectations, it does occasionally happen that a host and a guest agree to a booking but on the day of arrival, one of them changes their mind. A 24-hour cancellation policy applies to both hosts and guests.

If a guest shows up at their appointed lodging and finds it unsuitable, unclean, or different from what they'd envisioned from the pictures, Airbnb allows up to 24 hours from check-in time to call and notify them of any cancellations. A host is also granted the same opportunity to notify Airbnb within a day of check-in if they have an issue with a guest. I have no idea what would warrant such a need for a cancellation, and I have never heard any of my host friends say they've turned away a guest, but I am sure it does happen from time to time.

When either party needs to cancel before check-in, how much is refunded varies depending on the type of cancellation policy the host has in effect (or the duration of the booking). The company offers five types of cancellation policies: flexible, moderate, strict, super strict, and long-term. Both my listings are set to "moderate," allowing guests a full refund (less Airbnb fees) up to five days prior to arrival. This policy has served me well. For guests wanting to book (or hosts accepting) long-term stays—essentially a roommate situation—I highly suggest using the site's messaging and phone service to chat at length with your potential roommate before confirming a reservation so neither of you end up with a dud.

Nicola turned out to be a quiet, lovely, and unobtrusive roommate whom I rarely saw. She worked long hours and traveled out of state on occasion. Though Nicola had proclaimed a love of cooking and gardening, I never saw her in the kitchen or back yard. *So much for those raised vegetable beds and restoring my maple tree to health*, I thought. She ordered a pepperoni pizza every Saturday night and loved watching television alone in her room. Sometimes she'd come upstairs to hang out on the couch and watch her shows on her tiny laptop.

Occasionally, Alison and Alistair invited her to join them at neighborhood events. Nicola initially accepted their invitations, but often backed out at the last minute. In her, I saw a shyness I could relate to. I could empathize with her apparent loneliness, which seemed coupled with a still-hopeful optimism for future companionship. She loved watching Spanish telenovelas and stared at the screen with rapt attention. On occasion, Nicola talked about her background and her experiences moving from South America to Idaho, as well as her late-to-convert Mormonism. She noted, but did not lament, the restrictions it placed on her interactions with men.

Given her age, she said, the fact that she was unmarried made her a bit of an oddity at her esteemed Mormon college. Her Mormon sister had met and married a man in less than six months, and I sensed the romantic in Nicola fervently hoped for a similar fate. It was not uncommon, back at her college, for couples to meet and marry in only a few months' time. She said that even her professors openly teased her about her unmarried status. This seemed appalling to me, but it was something she seemed to take in stride, or simply didn't know how to fight back against.

Backing out of commitments to venture out with the Alison and Alistair meant she wasn't meeting anyone or making any local friends, but she maintained that her religion placed a lot of constraints on her. Talking to Nicola about men at her college was like talking to an adolescent in high school. I sensed her inexperience with men, and it seemed as if the thought of venturing out and interacting with men who didn't share her religion—away from the safety of her church or religious college community—frightened her.

I didn't judge Nicola's lifestyle and religion. I actually found her beliefs fascinating, because I'd never known or conversed with a Mormon. However, there was a part of me that wished more for her. I wished she could grow confident enough to challenge her professors when they teased her. Perhaps that same confidence would attract the husband she wanted so desperately. I sent a little juju into the Universe, hoping that she'd one day find a man who would give her the kind of love she imagined—and sighed about—as she curled up with her laptop alone in her bed.

FALL

"When the plane descended and we could see all the trees, were you thinking what I was thinking…that it would be nice to live here?" asked Rachel expectantly, smiling as she looked up at her husband. As his faced turned and dipped toward hers, Mark returned her look with a smile. As he met her gaze, Mark's eyes and subtle nod confirmed that he had also been thinking similar thoughts when their plane approached Sea-Tac Airport. They were sitting on the couch, each holding a champagne flute, though it was only ten in the morning.

I'd corresponded with Rachel a few times via email in advance of their arrival from San Francisco. They'd booked a one-week stay and were using the townhouse as a hub for their overnight trips to Portland, Oregon, and Vancouver, British Columbia. I was a bit surprised they'd booked the whole week, but I welcomed their money and the quiet that their every-other-day absence would offer me, while still adding to my checking account.

In her messages, Rachel asked if I could have a bottle of champagne chilling in their room when they arrived, and told me she'd be happy to reimburse me with cash. She wanted to surprise Mark in celebration of their ten-year anniversary. Other than the guest who'd requested her linens be washed in allergen-free detergent, I'd had no special requests since I opened my doors in April. I told Rachel I'd be more than happy to buy them a bottle of bubbly, gratis, in honor of their anniversary, and it would be waiting in their room.

Mark and Rachel were the most adorable married

couple under the age of sixty I've ever had the pleasure of meeting. Both in their early thirties, Mark was in great shape, a salt-and-pepper beard covering his handsome face, and Rachel was petite and slim, with long, curly brown hair and warm brown eyes.

That first morning we met, I came downstairs to the sound of Frank Sinatra playing on the record player. Mark was snapping his fingers to the rhythm and standing in front of the record player a few feet from Rachel, who was tucked snugly into the arm of the couch. They'd already popped their champagne. As a nod to their anniversary, I accepted their offer to join them in a celebratory glass. *The joys of freelancing at home*, I thought, taking a sip and taking a seat across from them in the living room.

Rachel gushed enthusiastically over my eclectic décor and asked if I had used a decorator. She said my place looked even better in person than it did in the online photos. I thanked her, and told her I didn't use a decorator, but loved trolling home décor websites like Apartment Therapy and House Beautiful. I also have a penchant for amassing books on interior design, as evidenced by the heavily-stacked book tower in my living room. A vertical tower in the shape of a spine that I bought from West Elm, it's a conversation piece in and of itself. People love to chat about the large design books and cocktail encyclopedias that anchor its base, their eyes gradually scanning up to the smaller, paperback Lonely Planet guides that finish off the top.

Airbnb strongly encourages hosts to post brightly lit photos of their home and to make an effort to highlight its best features. The company even offers their own photography service to hosts. Ideally, the primary photo should showcase the room the host is renting out.

Additional shots should show the bathroom (put that toilet seat down!) and offer a general sense of the home's interior. Listing a few photos of the surrounding neighborhood or nearby tourist attractions is a bonus, and can help market the place—especially if the area is of particular interest to visitors, like mine was. If you don't live near a lot of great tourist attractions, photograph interesting things in your home that give a guest a "feel" of the place. Things like an awesome spine book tower.

I was fortunate to have numerous friends who were professional photographers. Many were willing to photograph my place and help me as a friend, so I didn't need to utilize the photography service offered by Airbnb.

The best part about Airbnb's photography service when creating a new listing? It's generally free, if a host meets a few basic criteria—like living in a country where Airbnb has photographers, having a verified phone number and email address, and owning four or fewer listings. If a host qualifies, Airbnb will send a professional photographer out to photograph the host's home.

Another added benefit of the service is that because the photographer is arranged by Airbnb, the company is able to confirm that the house is just as it appears in photos. When the photographer uploads photos, also free of charge, they place a watermark over each picture that says, "Verified." It's kind of fun to visit the website and compare examples of hosts' "before" photos to the pros' "after" photos. I highly recommend taking advantage of this service if you qualify and live in a country where the benefit is offered.

A few days after our champagne meet-and-greet, Mark and Rachel returned from their overnight trip to Oregon. They arrived while I was hosting a dinner party with Hilary, a visiting friend from Los Angeles, and her local friend, Josh. Whenever my friends are visiting and end up interacting with my guests, I often get nervous, worrying that my guests will feel like they're intruding into my personal life. It's actually quite the opposite—I always want my guests to feel welcome and included, so I go to great lengths to ensure that welcome is conveyed.

On their way home, Mark and Rachel had stopped at the nearby Trader Joe's to stock up on wine and dinner items for the coming days. Our dinner party had diminished in size; some of our earlier guests had already left, so we had plenty of food remaining on the table and invited Mark and Rachel to join us. Grateful for the offer after the grueling, four-hour drive back from Portland on a Sunday night, they pulled up a chair and accepted our leftovers.

Over too much wine and diminishing reserves of food, we all shared stories from our past and present lives. Josh was a former Seattle colleague of Hilary's when she lived here, and she and I were newly acquainted. I hadn't met him before that evening. The next day, Josh said, he'd find out whether he'd been promoted into the upper echelons of Microsoft management. He felt confident he would. We all crookedly and drunkenly raised a glass to Josh in a pre-congratulatory toast, feeling just as sure of his promotion in that moment as he was.

Mark and Rachel talked about their life in California and how he was a mechanic and that they'd met at the dental office where she worked as the office manager. When she mailed Mark a routine follow-up postcard after his cleaning appointment, she wrote "Hope to see you soon!"—as in, for a dental visit—but he took it as a come-on and returned to the office well ahead of schedule to ask her out. She didn't remember him—or what she wrote on the postcard—but was impressed by his confidence and good looks and agreed to go out with him.

He took her to Disneyland on their first date. One year later, he proposed to her, also at Disneyland, on bended knee in front of Sleeping Beauty Castle and a bevy of applauding onlookers. I watched Rachel as Mark told the story they'd probably taken turns telling for the past decade. You could see in her smiling eyes that she loved hearing about her fairytale proposal and would likely never tire of the story—or her husband.

As the night turned to morning, Mark excused himself from the table and began preparing food in the kitchen. Their Trader Joe's provisions turned into our late-night drunken dining feast. Twenty minutes later, Mark placed a plate of food in front of every person at the table. Each plate featured a cheese quesadilla in the shape of Pac-Man, with eyes made of capers and a generous dab of guacamole in the cut-away wedge of his mouth. I smiled to myself, keenly aware of the moment and honored to be making such wonderful memories in my home, surrounded by an old friend and a few new ones.

That night at the table bonded us. We were no longer simply a host and her guests. In the remaining days of Mark and Rachel's visit, I toured them around Seattle in my SUV and showed them all of my favorite landmarks, ones that few tourists know about or have time to take in during a weekend visit.

On the day of their departure, Mark and Rachel packed their bags and prepared to head to the airport. Because it had been so many days since they'd used their rental car, Rachel couldn't find the keys. I watched helplessly as she frantically looked through her pockets and all their luggage. She was on the verge of tears, worried the keys' disappearance was her fault. The whole time she searched, Mark spoke calmly to her and reassured her that everything would be fine.

Watching them work through this mini-crisis was another fly-on-the-wall experience, and a chance to unobtrusively witness how folks interact behind closed doors in the mock comfort of home. Seeing how someone acts when they're stressed is one of the true insights into a person's character. The polite and respectful way Mark and Rachel spoke to one another, even under stress, confirmed to me they were as great a couple as I'd suspected during the week of getting to know them.

The fairytale couple who got engaged at Disneyland came to Seattle to celebrate their first ten years together. After getting to know Mark and Rachel, I have no doubt their happily-ever-after will last another fifty. During their stay, they showed me more than mere kindness with that first glass of champagne or the thoughtfully prepared Pac-Man meal. They showed me how a healthy couple can look when a pair is well-matched, in love, and practices kindness toward one other. It's rare for me to look around and see married friends whose marriages I hope to someday emulate. Mark and Rachel changed that, and we are still friends today. We're discussing a fall trip to Sonoma, right around the time they'll be celebrating their eleventh anniversary. I can't wait to raise another glass to them.

KANSAS CITY

10.7.2013

I knew I was in for an interesting experience the morning after I confirmed Linda's reservation. When I first saw her in a photo—a stoic-looking, retired chaplain from Kansas City—I thought her beautiful. She had a great face, and looked to me like someone who'd be spiritually interesting to meet and share conversation with. But much to my chagrin, in the three-week interval between her booking and arrival, Linda and I exchanged thirteen emails and six phone calls. This did not bode well and made me anxious about what to expect when she eventually arrived.

When Linda finally landed, on a cold, rainy Wednesday, she immediately began apprising me of her every movement as she made her way north to the city. "I'm on the train," she reported, from the Central Link light rail that zips commuters and travelers from Sea-Tac Airport to the Westlake Station downtown. An hour later: "I decided to take the bus, not a taxi; I'll be there shortly. Gosh, it's cold here. I am freezing." Ten minutes later: "Hi again, it's Linda. Gee, there's a lot of traffic. Are you going to be there when I arrive?" Quickly understanding that she needed extra hand-holding, I decided that instead of going to the gym, I would kill time in the living room and wait for her.

She coded her way in at the front door and came clumping up the stairs in a blustery mess. I was startled to see her platinum white hair that betrayed the younger, strawberry-blonde woman portrayed in her profile picture. The photo she posted on Airbnb had to have been taken at least fifteen years prior. As Linda dramatically struggled with her large carry-on, I introduced myself, calmly took her bag from her, and escorted her to her third-floor room. Once inside, she dropped her handbag on the bed and too-quickly accepted my offer of a cup of tea to warm her.

As the two of us sat in my living room, sans TV and electronic distraction, I felt grateful for one of the conscious choices I made when putting my personal touches on the design of the place. In my house, I have set up what my grandma would call a "parlor." It's stocked with board games, decks of cards, magazines, books, and records for the record player. It brings to mind a yesteryear I glimpse less and less in the frenetic pace of the modern day. Since moving in, it's become a place where wonderful conversations unfold.

Linda and I settled in front of the gas fireplace with our mugs of tea and chatted a bit about her life in Kansas City and why she was selling her home of thirty-five years to move to the Pacific Northwest. In that half-hour conversation, I learned a lot about the chaplain's life. No husband. No children. Thirty years as a recovering alco-holic. Retired from her service in the care of others, she came to the Northwest looking for "community." She feels most at home on islands, be them far-flung in foreign lands or respites from the mainland on native shores. She wants to live out her remaining days in a home surrounded by water. In the Northwest, she said she hoped to find a fellowship of likeminded, liberal people, which she hadn't yet found in Kansas City.

When I initially confirmed Linda's reservation and fielded her onslaught of emails, I suspected she might be anxious and a bit awkward. This brief, fireside conversation quickly confirmed that impression, and made me wonder if she turned people off back home. Thirty-five years in the same place, and she has to journey over two thousand miles to find community? I felt sorry for her and wanted to ensure she felt comfortable her first night in Seattle, so I made up a tale about needing to check out a new restaurant on Broadway and asked if she'd like to join me. She happily accepted, and a half hour later we settled in at a table in the darkened dining room of an Indian-Tibetan restaurant up the street from the house.

Within minutes of our food arriving at the table, Linda said she felt sick and seemed kind of out of it. Her skin tone had changed from rosy pink to a milky-white pallor, a tone that almost matched her hair, and she was swaying a bit. I encouraged her to drink some water, while I beckoned the waiter and asked him to bag our food. He looked at me strangely, as if something was wrong with the meal, and I assured him everything was lovely but something had suddenly come up. I quickly paid the bill and ushered Linda outside. It immediately became clear she was unable to walk the few blocks back to the house, so she asked if I could hail a taxi.

In that moment, arms laden with still-warm food, I'd never been so grateful for my ability to whistle with no fingers and attempt to hail a cab. Occupied cabs passed us by, and I worried what I would do if Linda fainted. Given her age and knowing very little about her background, I wondered if she was seriously ill or perhaps suffered from diabetes or bouts of low blood pressure. Just when I began to despair we'd never find a taxi in time, a cab driver met my eyes from across the street as he was driving the opposite direction. He made an illegal U-turn to stop in front of the restaurant. The cabbie told me that even from across the street he could see the desperation in my eyes. It chilled me that this astute driver could see my fear, and I considered him a godsend.

Arriving home, I opened the front door and followed Linda up the stairs to the third floor. She collapsed on the bed amid my offer to open windows, start a fan, and get her a glass of water from the kitchen. When I returned two minutes later with the water, I paused in the doorway when I saw her, frail and shirtless on the bed.

A person, who was a stranger to me two hours before, was now relying on me for care. It struck me that I was forever acting the daughter, primed in my mind to one day care for my mother, in the same way that I was now helping this stranger. Except this stranger, I realized, is daughterless, which viscerally saddened me at a gut level. A heartbeat of a second later, I became acutely aware that I am also daughterless. In this woman, I saw myself. Thirty years from now, I could be her if I continued to be single and childless. It was a terrifying thought to entertain that strange evening and in the days afterward.

Was Linda seeking community now, while she was still relatively physically adept, in an effort to form attachments with people who would hopefully one day care for her? Is that what happens to people with no spouse, no living relatives, and no children? I wondered if it was Linda's anxieties about her future that made her act so awkwardly now, or was it those same anxieties that had prevented her from bonding with a partner long ago?

Those future fears I recognized when I was speaking with Jackie from Reno and Julie from Denver reared their ugly heads again when I thought about Linda. There's a thread that connects us all, but that same thread also serves as the fine line many of us walk—I know I do—toward a regrettable future we may not want to sign up for.

Strangers from around the world visit my home and

constantly remind me of the universality of the human condition—how we are alike in a lot of ways. Linda came along and taught me so much about a future I don't want for myself. That realization crushed me like the weight of a ton of bricks. Sometimes that's the nature of the people who walk through my door and the lessons they unwittingly teach me.

IMPOSSIBLE TO PLEASE

10.24.13

As summer turned into fall and the high season of summer dissipated, I noticed a marked drop-off in my bookings. I had set my summer rate, apart from the two-month stays of the summer interns, at $85 a night, and at this price, so far there had been no problem booking guests and filling my rooms from June through the end of September.

Because I live in an immensely desirable city with a lot of tourist attractions, conventions, and stunning recreational offerings, hotels charge premium rates here. By all accounts, the rate that a host on Airbnb is able to offer a tourist (even during high season) is going to be a whole lot cheaper than a downtown hotel and will offer a much more personal experience. Affordable, personable, and effortless—these are the most common terms my guests use to describe their experiences using Airbnb.

Getting used to being rated by dozens of people on who you are as a person and as a host took some getting used to. In the community that is the Airbnb marketplace, how you present yourself is often just as important as what you're offering under your roof. It was gratifying and confidence-boosting to read that people especially appreciated the tips I could offer about Seattle because of my tenure in real estate and my longtime resident status.

The number of Airbnb reviews from my guests had climbed into the thirties for each room, and several would-be guests noted the apparent desirability (according to reviews from former guests) of my listings. I was humbled by all of the kind things people had to say about me and my home. These reviews are a great asset and an important selling feature when attracting future guests.

I find that the strength of online reviews carries a lot of weight when a guest is deciding whether to book with one host versus another. From personal experience as a guest, I've found that the fewer reviews a host has, the less seasoned they are to guests' needs. That being said, everyone has to start somewhere. Every host starts with zero reviews. Learning how to host effectively and garner great reviews involves a learning curve—and every host will become better attuned to guests' needs the more they deal with visitors.

After the debacle with the Korean family, I also abandoned my weekly rates in favor of nightly and monthly rates only. Perhaps it was hubris for me to abandon my weekly rates, but I also had grown confident in what I had to offer as a host, and in the demand for my location. I didn't want to attract a "hostel" type of guest that was looking for cheap lodging and would probably treat my home with less care. I wanted to attract a higher-caliber guest, so I set my rates accordingly, and it seemed to work. My off-season rates went down to $75 per night, starting on October 1st.

Since it was still my first full season as a host, I hadn't known to expect the summer intern rush, nor had I figured out exactly when I could expect the tourist season to taper off. In the fall, as student travelers returned to their colleges and the weather in Seattle grew markedly more dismal, I noticed a major decrease in bookings, beginning in October. High and low seasons are different for every host, depending on location, year-round attractions, and weather. Seattle, infamous for its rain, is not really all that rainy. But locals don't like to tell the rest of the world that, lest more people decide to move here.

In mid-October, looking at a bleak calendar with weeks of vacant rooms on the horizon, I received an email from a Russian woman. She lived in New Jersey with her American-born husband and they were considering staying with me for two weeks. The couple planned to relocate to Seattle in December and wanted a home base so they could look for an apartment at a leisurely pace. She asked if I would give them a flat rate for the two weeks.

I always respect people who are willing to negotiate or at least ask for a reduction. It doesn't hurt to try. I won't acquiesce on my pricing in summer, but since I wasn't sure what my winter months would look like, I offered the woman a two-week flat rate at about a 20% discount from my halved monthly rate. Airbnb lets hosts send special offers to guests if they prefer to lower their stated rate. This can be handy if a host wants to reward a return guest, offer a lower rate than stated, or if the person was referred by a friend or family member. The Russian woman snapped up the discounted offer and promptly booked my third-floor room.

The couple seemed amicable enough when we first met. We chatted about where they lived and what they were looking forward to about moving to Seattle. They wanted to find a modern apartment, and I assured them that with the recent influx of Amazon employees and a host of booming new construction projects, they'd surely find a wonderful, contemporary place to live.

They didn't. Each night I'd come home to the woman standing in the kitchen, making tea and lamenting the undesirable Seattle apartment offerings. Nothing was good enough for her. And her husband? He was another handful, making a point to tell me he went to the store and bought organic sugar to replace the granulated white sugar I kept in the cupboard. I suspected he was gay, which may have been why his wife seemed so uptight. I also thought she might be an online "mail-order" bride, underwhelmed by him and the life he'd given her in America.

This couple *loved* to shower. *A lot*. Never together, but between the hours of 11:00 p.m. and 1:00 a.m. it was not uncommon to hear the shower running for long stretches of time, and then some quiet, until it would start up again. I often wear earplugs to bed so I can sleep through the slamming of doors or my guests' late-night showering habits, but these two took the cake. I figured a good chunk of their flat-rate fee would be paying my upcoming water bill.

One night, in an effort to dull the late-night sounds coming out of their bedroom (not those ones!) and bathroom, I turned on the fan in my master bathroom. My bathroom separated the two rooms and served as a pretty decent sound barrier. At four in the morning, I awoke with a start to the sound of a text message dinging on my phone. The couple next door were texting me to turn off the bathroom fan! No please, no question marks. Just a command. Pissed at the intrusion, I lay in bed and debated whether I should acknowledge their rudeness. Ten minutes later, when I hadn't yet turned off the fan, they texted again! *Assholes!*

Fuming, I finally acquiesced, got up and turned off the fan, and never spoke to them again for the remaining five days of their stay. I have a big house, and I work in my writing loft a lot during the day. Most evenings, I like to go out. When they weren't out in the city scoping out apartments—ones that would never be good enough—they never left their room. So it wasn't as difficult as you might think to avoid contact. I am not proud to admit this moment in my hosting history, but I've always been uncomfortable with confrontation. Assertiveness was another personal attribute I was in the process of working on during my first year as a host. Clearly, I wasn't there yet.

The hard-to-please couple became one of two go-to stories I tell people who wonder if I'd ever had any "bad" experiences as a host. As you can see, it's nothing egregious, simply an awkward and odd situation caused by a couple of unhappy and inconsiderate people. I consider myself lucky that thus far, they're the worst people I've had to contend with on my journey as a host.

WINTER

12.21.13

In late November, my tenants had moved out of my former home in Green Lake, so I decided to put it on the market. It was achingly heartbreaking to put my first house up for sale, and at one point I thought I'd have to go on anxiety medication.

I'd been so proud to be a twenty-six-year-old homeowner and to march rank and file with my realtor coworkers in making savvy investment decisions. But in truth, I also bought the house as an emotional investment in a future that never materialized. It was painful to look around a beautiful house that was a "smart investment" but didn't feel like a home. It was time to release the past and let it go. The house sold in three days.

To celebrate the closing of the house and to give closure to that often sad chapter of my life, I decided to book a trip to Europe. Michelle, a fellow freelancer, joined me for an eleven-day trip to Amsterdam, Prague, and Paris. It was a spur-of-the-moment decision, and it would be a whirlwind trip, but I saw it as an important step toward creating a new life on my own terms.

I was curious to use Airbnb as a guest, and I was looking forward to experiencing the other side of the booking equation. As we prepared for the trip, looking at listings and interacting with hosts gave me a little bit of insight into how others handled their businesses. It also gave me a dose of empathy for guests.

It's easy to become impatient while a host decides whether or not to accept your reservation, or even to acknowledge your inquiry. I am sure this communication guessing game is what compels a lot of hosts and guests to use the "Instant Book" feature, but I am staunchly against it. I use the friendliness of the introductory email as a litmus test of whether to accept a guest, or, from the perspective of a guest, whether to book with a particular host. I like this extra level of security and ability to dialogue and build rapport before confirming a reservation.

Airbnb has an algorithm listed below a host's picture that tells you what their response rate is, how long it takes them to answer messages (a few hours to a few days), and how recently their calendar has been updated. This is all very helpful information if you're trying to gauge if a host's calendar is up to date for the dates you're interested in, and the scoring system lets you know how quickly you can expect a response. I found the rating to be very accurate in my dealings with European hosts, and I appreciate the upfront expectation set by the algorithm.

Something else to keep in mind when navigating the Airbnb marketplace is that time zones and language fluency must be taken into consideration if you're booking with a guest or host from another country. The site does a good job helping to make communication easier by offering language translation as part of their messaging and listing platform.

Before booking our last-minute trip, I'd already accepted a five-day reservation for my ground-floor room during the same time period. I really didn't want to cancel on Melody and Ian, the Florida couple who had booked the room. In emails we exchanged before she confirmed the booking, Melody said she and Ian had been offered a free trip through his work, and they were greatly looking forward to the opportunity to leave their five kids with family. Neither of them had ever been to the Northwest.

Coming from the heat of Southern Florida, Melody couldn't wait to experience cold temperatures, possibly even snow, and the holiday festivities in a big city.

Immediately after I confirmed my European trip, I contacted Melody and asked if she felt okay that I would not be home during their five-day visit. I assured her it was fine with me if she and Ian enjoyed the house while I was gone, and told her I would have a friend available to take care of any issues or needs that came up during their stay. Melody assured me it wasn't a problem and wished me a safe trip and wonderful holiday season.

Though I was excited to get out of town, I had some anxiety about leaving the house in the hands of total strangers without being around to oversee the day-to-day nuances of having people in my home. It was my first time doing so, and while I was willing to take the risk in order to escape to Europe, I wondered how it would turn out.

Over time, I noticed I'd grown more comfortable having people in my house and more trusting they'd be polite and well-behaved in my space. But there was still a small part of me that knew the couple's experience would be different—and maybe not as good—without me there. I worried about things like not being able to make sure Melody and Ian were comfortable, and being unable to steer them to all the best tourist sites. I also fretted over practical matters, like hoping they'd remember to turn off the stove so they didn't burn the house to the ground. I was an anxious, detail-oriented people-pleaser, now in the process of becoming a recovering one. Remember when I speculated about why I'd spent most of my adult life alone?

Before heading to the airport, on my way out I left Melody and Ian a note with my friend Dan's phone number in case of an emergency. I told them to use the fireplace, listen to records, make dinners in the kitchen, and basically treat the home like it was their own while I was away.

When I returned from my trip eleven days later, it was more than just a little disconcerting to find empty beer and wine bottles filling the recycling bins and trash. We're talking an amount of empties that would make a frat boy blush. I called Dan who, in addition to being on hand if Melody and Ian needed anything, had also watched the house. I asked if he'd perhaps stayed over and gone on a bit of a bender. He said he had not stayed over, but had checked on things after Melody and Ian left, and everything looked fine to him.

Melody and Ian had obviously taken me up on my advice to enjoy my home as if it was theirs. Their home was an open bar, apparently. As I rinsed the bottles for the curbside recycling bins, I noticed the bottles in the kitchen bins were a mix of what must have been beers they'd purchased, as well as all the beers from my fridge and some of the wine from my wine rack! I was glad I'd been prescient enough to hide all my hard alcohol in a high cupboard because I suspect half of that would have been missing too.

Alcohol is a tricky thing to have in the house on full display. Coming from a long line of alcoholics, I am sensitive to having booze visible to those who might struggle with seeing it around the house. I'm an extreme craft cocktail enthusiast, but I've even tucked away the vintage alcohol posters I used to love displaying in my home for fear of offending a guest.

Hosts, ask yourself if you want people to drink your sauce without you offering it to them. Because guests just might, if it's out and visible. You may want to have language in your House Rules that explicitly mentions alcohol consumption—what's offered gratis in your home and what is not. Hide your alcohol in your room or in high cupboards if you're at all worried about it.

Other than Melody and Ian who took my advice and made themselves a little *too* comfortable, I have had only one other person drink my booze (some expensive, unopened vodka I'd forgotten about in the freezer) without my permission. If you're a guest, let this serve as a warning—you shouldn't drink a host's alcohol without their express permission. It's a no-no.

All that being said, there are few host moments I love more than offering a bottle of wine to a guest or opening up a bottle to share with them over conversation (once I've surmised they're okay with the sauce). I have also seen listings in regions renowned for their wine—places like France, Italy, Oregon, and Northern California—where hosts leave a complimentary bottle of wine in guests' rooms. It's a lovely gesture, but if you think you might want to offer this to guests, consider if you'd be okay with spillage on your carpets or the possibility of offending a recovering alcoholic. Just some booze for thought.

The situation with Melody and Ian was odd, but not devastating. In their wake of bottles in the bins and too-warm-for-Florida clothes left in their room, they left me a gorgeous orchid plant. Next to this beautiful gift was a handwritten note thanking me for the wonderful time they'd had in my home. Having noticed my love of exotic plants, Melody thought I'd enjoy another one. I was grateful for the gift, but since she was a first-time user of the site, I was left wondering if I should contact Melody about the tackiness of drinking a host's booze without asking.

Twenty-four hours after a guest checks out, an email arrives asking both the host and the guest to leave one another a public review and to rate their experience. Each party has thirty days to write a review of their experience. The site also allows both hosts and guests an opportunity to give private feedback to each other, away from the public eye. If I had been home when Melody and Ian left, this would have been my chance to notify Melody of their error in social graces. The site recently added an option that allows users to send Airbnb private feedback about a particular guest or host if a person wants to notify the company (but not the other party) of any issues. Personally, I've never needed to tell Airbnb something about a guest I couldn't tell the guest directly.

In the spirit, ahem, "spirits" of the season, even though I still had the thirty-day window to write a review and give Melody private feedback, I ultimately decided against saying anything. I've given up worrying about whether I should play moral policewoman and follow up with guests about their mistakes or shortcomings. I learned from the experience, so instead of hassling the couple about it after the fact, I figure they can contend with future hosts' flexibility and House Rules.

Because we're all so different, I know that I offer only one perspective. I'm grateful to for the opportunity to invite wonderful people into my house. And about 99% of them are fantastic. So for the rare occasions when there's trouble (or maybe just a bit of an odd situation) I deal with it sympathetically, as if the person did not know better, and then I move on.

PROVENCE

The strains of Kenny Rogers' *Lucille* fill my home as I walk in my front door and head up the stairs to the living room. This record always reminds me of drives in my father's pickup truck. Dad at the wheel and my older brother on my right, with me sandwiched happily between the first two pivotal men in my life. Classical and Motown music were fine at home, but country was the only genre my dad allowed in his Chevy. George Strait, Alabama, Waylon Jennings—those were the greats who accompanied us on our weekend errand-running.

I round the corner at the top of my stairs and see Julien, a handsome, 25-year-old Frenchman from Provence standing at my kitchen counter.

"Oh, hello," he greets me warmly in deliciously accented English.

"You've discovered my records," I say as I glance to my right and see Frank Sinatra and Elvis lined up next to Kenny on the side table, waiting their turn to wow Julien and his girlfriend Sylvie with some nostalgic Americana.

"Are you liking this old music?" I ask.

Julien smiles widely, "Yes, very much. My sister's name is Lucile, but only with one 'l.' I have never heard of this song."

It's my turn to smile.

I love it that these inexpensive records bring so much pleasure to my guests. They take me back in time to my childhood, and they offer my foreign guests a chance to have an "authentic" experience with older American music. I suppose I could be deluding them to some extent, because

I suspect few people play the Bee Gees, Joni Mitchell, Carly Simon, and Van Morrison on vinyl in their homes anymore. I have these records because they're sold everywhere in my neighborhood—at thrift shops and in the $1 discount crates at the used record store.

In offering these records, and this somewhat make-believe experience for my guests, I provide them with a glimpse of what America used to look like through the ribbed lens of vinyl. Like the roaming French opera singers I saw performing *Carmen* at a hidden park in the Marais district of Paris two weeks ago, they also performed for the tourists' benefit—cultured busking, if you will. Though it was contrived, it was lovely; I couldn't have been more grateful to stumble upon the singers. So even though my records and turntable represent another put-on performance of sorts, I am glad to act as unofficial conductor and conduit to my guests' "American" experience.

Admittedly, this somewhat atypical music offering leads to some pretty memorable conversations. My guests, especially the young ones from other countries, come here with grand notions about American music—about Michael Jackson, Elvis Presley, and Lady Gaga. I do my part to dispel myths and confirm truths, though I am no expert. Since Seattle is such a hotbed for music—and the home of ground-breaking artists like Jimi Hendrix, Nirvana, Pearl Jam, and Soundgarden—it's a frequent topic of conversation in my home. It turns out Julien is a DJ back home in Provence on weekends, when he's not working his day-to-day grind as an architect. He loves spinning records but had never seen 90% of my collection in the record stores back in France.

One evening during their stay, Julien offered to cook

me a "humble" French meal he had learned to make as a child. He said it was not uncommon for French children to start cooking by the age of six or seven. Julien said when he was a young boy, his aunts, uncles, and grandparents would stand around the kitchen watching him cook. When he was finished, they'd offer feedback on his technique and the food. I was horrified to learn of this off-the-cuff panel of family judges critiquing a little boy, but Julien said he felt blessed, and that their input helped him improve his technique and refine his palate. It was how his family bonded and passed down family recipes and culinary techniques. Back home in Provence, Julien loves cooking for Sylvie in the apartment they share, and she's happy to let him because she hates cooking.

When Julien set the peasant omelet, roasted duck, red potatoes with goat cheese, and decadent strawberry tartlet in front of me, my jaw dropped. *This was humble?* Everything was unbelievably delicious.

Wanting to extend my thanks to him in a way that would parallel his memorable offering to me, I gave him the Kenny Rogers album. I knew a dollar would buy me another album, but the gift would be as priceless to him as his meal had been to me.

Guests like Julien and Sylvie are not necessarily a rarity, but I like to honor the pinch-me-is-this-really-my-life feeling that has become my new normal. The night they left, I fired up the turntable and reminisced about the old days in my dad's pickup.

MINNESOTA

The family reminded me of the Berenstain Bears, sans the bib overalls. Exuding warmth, kindness, and familial love, John and June were the kind of people I wanted to hug instead of shake hands with upon introduction. Their daughter, Anna, just finished college and recently started her first big-girl job in the city. Brother Billy was home in Minnesota watching Jasper, the family dog. Billy had already sent his mom a video update—I know this because June showed me the video he had taken of the boisterous collie romping around their family room.

John and June had been itching to come out to verify in person that their daughter was doing okay. Anna had settled into city life nicely, and had already found a sweet boyfriend. I sensed that Mama and Papa really just missed their little girl, who wasn't so little anymore.

John couldn't quite believe that the low, low price they paid for the room afforded them use of my kitchen, dining room, and cozy living room. It was the family's first time using Airbnb. They were a little cautious in their inquiry about inviting Anna over, perhaps fearing I might say no, but were thrilled when I assured them it would be fine for her to visit the house anytime. After the debacle with the South Korean family, whose grown son had camped out for a week, having Anna over for dinner seemed like a walk in the park. As long as I didn't need to perform another tipsy Operation Towel Drop, I was happy to accommodate the sweet family.

Unlike staying in a hotel room and being forced to maneuver around beds, meet in the lobby, or pay a higher rate for a suite with a seating area in order to hang out together, the open layout of my house allowed the Berenstains to comfortably connect with their daughter.

Bonding with friends or family in a host's home, as if you were actually in your own home, is one of the incalculable benefits of using Airbnb over a standard hotel. No offense to the hoteliers of the world. Sterile hotel rooms are fine for folks celebrating a special getaway or who want the assurance of a corporate standard, but most Airbnb users are interested in a more personal experience. I know there are innumerable lodging options—from quaint motels to huge skyscrapers—and I'd like to believe there's enough of a tourism market to support everyone's preferences.

Traditional hotels are great for the average traveler, but the home-sharing traveler is a new breed. Dare I say a more adventurous one? Airbnb is not yet offered in every city worldwide, but their network of lodging options is growing every day. As of this writing, in June of 2014, the Airbnb marketplace has listings in 34,000 cities and 190 countries.

Airbnb offers affordability and a non-vanilla, non-corporate stay. Comparing Airbnb offerings to the variations in the hotel experience is not black and white. The Airbnb experience is not for everyone, but it does provide a break from the norm of a typical hotel room or suite. The adventure of the quirky place where you're going to rest your head at night is almost as much of a curiosity and something to look forward to as to the sights you'll see on your trip. So far, over fifteen million nightly stays have been booked via Airbnb. The model is obviously resonating with people.

I've found most of my guests are savvy people who

aren't necessarily "budget" travelers, but are folks looking to meet and connect with others when they visit a place. These intrepid travelers like to meet local people like me or their friends and family who live in the area. As a frequent traveler myself, and based on my conversations with dozens of fellow travelers, I believe affordability and the ability to foster personal interactions with locals are the two biggest lures that draw guests away from traditional hotels. Airbnb provides both.

Naturally, hotels don't like this, and are starting to pressure city officials about the impact that home-sharing sites like Airbnb are having on hotel tourism and the rental economy. Residents in highly desirable cities are finding fewer rental offerings as landlords choose to do short-term rentals through home-sharing sites rather than locking in long-term tenants. Short-term stays garner higher returns than long-term tenants, so you can see why a landlord might embrace the home-sharing model. All you have to do is a simple Google search or read the occasional headline in the *New York Times* or the *San Francisco Chronicle* to see how judicial agencies and the hotel industry in those two cities are dealing with Airbnb's growing presence. I'll leave you to your own Internet search and inquiry on that one. I'd need another whole book to cover that subject in depth.

In addition to affordability and comfort, there's also the voyeuristic lure of wanting to play looky-loo in the home of a local. I remember my first visit to Paris in December of 2005. When it grew dark in the pre-dinner hours, I would wander the streets, craning my neck to look into brightly lit apartments with heavy curtains and soaring, ornate ceilings. I was dying to learn more about typical Parisians and to discover what an everyday interior looked like. I had hoped (more than I'd wished for a friendly French waiter) I could befriend some locals and beg my way into their apartment.

When I went back to Paris in 2013, I got my wish—without having to grovel or attempt to use my poor French. There was an abundance of gorgeous Parisian lodging options on Airbnb, but since I'd never stayed in the eighteenth arrondissement, I booked a room with a sweet couple in Montmartre. The boyfriend, a writer, worked from home during the day while his architect girlfriend was away at work. He met my friend and I at the door of their historic building in a sketchy part of town located near the Barbès-Rochechouart subway stop.

The old apartment—with its ancient circular wooden staircase, decrepit elevator, rear servants' entry into the kitchen, flourished marble fireplace, and fifteen-foot ceilings—did not disappoint. If I had been in Paris longer, I might have chosen to book multiple stays with different hosts, just to sample the various Parisian interiors.

The second night of John and June's stay, I rounded the top of my first-floor staircase and found the family resting comfortably in the living room. Anna was sprawled out on the floor in front of the fireplace, her legs kicked up on the coffee table—a teenage pose that belied her twenty-three years. Anna's boyfriend, a gangly man in his early twenties with a mop of curly dark hair and mild acne, sat stiffly on the couch in front of John. Before shaking my hand with his own moist one, he'd been absentmindedly picking his nails and tapping his foot. I don't know what made him more nervous—being in a stranger's house or talking with Anna's dad.

John was nestled in the overstuffed leather armchair, comfortable as a clam and looking besotted that he had both his girls in one place. I think he also secretly enjoyed the fact that Anna's young suitor was nervous. Anna, obviously accustomed to her father's antics, was ignoring the pair and appeared to be more interested her smartphone. As I walked toward the kitchen, I listened as the young man stammered out answers to John about his job and living situation. I think John was pretend hinting he'd like to see the boy propose to Anna, even though the couple had met only three months prior. I could tell by the laughter in John's voice that his humor was good old-fashioned fatherly ribbing, but based on the sweat beading on the young man's brow and the terrified look on his face, I don't think the poor kid was getting the joke.

June was wrapping up leftovers in the kitchen and asked if she could make me a plate before she put everything away. I accepted her offer, and as I stood at the kitchen counter, picking at my plate, June told me about their life in Minnesota—how John worked as an accountant and how she'd been a stay-at-home mom since Anna was born. When Anna and Billy were young, nothing made June happier than having an apron around her waist, a house full of the kids' friends, and something cooking on the stove or baking in the oven.

The family's story was the perfect snapshot of middle-class America, but I'd had little contact with such a nurturing existence. Growing up as a latchkey kid after my parents divorced, June described a life completely foreign to the one I'd known. I was envious of the picture she painted with her words while I ate my leftover mashed potatoes and cold chicken. Watching the wholesome family in my home, I could easily envision them in their own home back in the Midwest.

It's amazing how quickly people can get comfortable

in a place, once they are together with their friends or family. It doesn't much matter that they aren't at home, because it's the being together that matters.

It's a surreal feeling to step into an intimate moment in the lives of virtual strangers. Sometimes you'll catch a glimpse of their authentic selves, a hidden view, far removed from the performance most of us put on in public. Of course, they've also voluntarily stepped into my world, my once-private space.

The Airbnb model and the home-sharing economy have turned the concept of home on its head. As we progress into the twenty-first century, what will home mean to us as more and more people shed the boundaries of our personal space? It's certainly an evolution, and some would say a home revolution. Home used to be the only refuge many of us had from the outside world. Until now.

It's a not always easy to share your home with strangers—and it's something that takes effort and open-mindedness—but it can most certainly be done. As a host, being able to entertain strangers is an unusual gift. A gift in the sense that it takes talent, but also in the reward I get from hosting. I give, but I get so much more in return. With every guest who walks through my door, the landscape of my literal and emotional interior is continually changing…and evolving.

KNOXVILLE

Culler and Roxanne are very different from my local friends. Even with women I have known for a decade, I often feel the icy drafts of the chilly "Seattle Freeze" the city is known for. Seattle locals and recent transplants are quick to talk about "Seattle Nice," with the stress on "ice." It's common for people to be warm and friendly to your face, promising to connect with you after that first meeting. But the follow-through of actually seeing them again? It's as rare as a 100-degee day 'round these parts. Even if you do connect, people are often superficially friendly, but I've learned not to expect them to get too close. Having lived here so long, I am guilty of some of the same inclinations, at times.

People speculate it's the infamous weather and residents' tendencies to want to stay indoors and read a book or surf online that makes them so awkward when it comes to face-to-face interaction. But the Freeze is a very real problem in this city. You're left to wonder, is it the chicken or the egg that came first? Do depressed people move here, or does the city make people depressed and withdrawn? That's not to say that Seattle is a town full of friendless people—folks eventually connect and make strong friendships, it just seems to take a little more effort and commitment to make it happen.

I don't know if it's Culler and Roxanne's laid-back, hospitable southern vibe or their willingness to share parts of themselves—I can't put my finger on it—but these women are special.

I first met Culler and Roxanne in October of 2013

when they booked a four-day stay. After a long day of traveling from their respective homes in Knoxville, Tennessee, they landed late on a Thursday night. Their friends back home wondered why they chose Seattle for their West Coast getaway instead of Los Angeles or Portland. It was Seattle's rock music history and liberal attitude that drew them here, they said. They felt an undeniable and unexplainable attraction to the city, and had grown tired of constantly explaining their reasons to their friends.

After that first night, when I said hello and made sure they were settled comfortably, I didn't see them again until their last day, when the pair invited me to meet them for happy hour before their late-evening departure. I was accustomed to guests inviting me out, and since they seemed nice and their happy hour offer was on my way to another event, I accepted.

Over beers, they told me stories of their whirlwind weekend. On Friday, they'd met two Microsoft guys who'd offered to play tour guide and show them around town. The foursome took the ferry across the Sound to Bainbridge Island; stopped at Kerry Park on Queen Anne Hill for the renowned evening views of the city, mountains, and Sound; and ate and drank their way through some of city's newest restaurants.

Culler was a beautiful, willowy actress with shoulder-length blonde hair. Roxanne was a gorgeous, red-headed speech therapist. They were both intelligent and charismatic. I could see why the Microsoft guys picked them up at Linda's, a renowned local dive bar, and wanted to spend time as much time with them as possible before they had to part ways.

The gentlemen knew Roxanne had a boyfriend, but

they didn't care. Culler was single, and I could tell she was accustomed to male attention. She shrugged off my query into the guys' motivations as casually as one would dismiss someone asking you if you thought it would rain today. Their interest didn't seem to matter to her either way, and I admired her nonchalance when it came to the opposite sex. As a bookish and awkward nerd, meeting new men was something I had never navigated with much confidence or ease.

The Microsoft guys told the women they simply enjoyed their company, especially their lack of jadedness, which they saw as a refreshing change from the average, bored hipster they were accustomed to meeting in Capitol Hill bars. As I talked to Culler and Roxanne, I could tell what the Microsoft fellas meant. These effusive, charming women were a breath of fresh air in a city whose denizens exuded calculated disinterest, apathy, and remove.

While the Microsoft guys were no doubt falling for the women, Culler and Roxanne had fallen for Seattle, saying it was so different from Knoxville. They were so smitten they told me they hoped to move to Seattle the following summer. I encouraged them to do so and to look me up if they needed a place to stay again or wanted advice on where to live. Even as I said it, I recognized a little of my own Seattle jadedness pawing its emerald claws into the offer, believing I'd likely never hear from them. I finished my beer, and as I stood, preparing to say goodbye, Culler slipped me a greeting card with a handwritten note of thanks from both of them inside.

A card with a heartfelt a personal note inside is one of my all-time favorite gifts to receive. I love words. I love snail mail. I love postage stamps. Getting a card in person card is the next best thing to finding something other than a bill in my mailbox. And more than anything, I love knowing that the person took the time to pick up a card because they cared about me or appreciated something I did for them. Culler loved cards, too, and told me she made intricate cards by hand and sold them in indie stores back home. I asked her to mail me one and promised I'd send them both some postcards from Seattle from time to time if it would bolster their desire to move.

I walked out of the bar honestly expecting never to hear from Culler and Roxanne again. But I was wrong.

A few days after they left, I received one of Culler's handmade cards in the mail. A couple of months later, at Christmas, another handmade card arrived from Knoxville. By that time, we'd also become friends on Facebook, and Culler and Roxanne loved seeing my pictures and posts about Seattle. With my background in real estate and long tenure in the city, friends around the world considered me a bit of an expert on the city. In online messages and snail-mail postcards featuring quirky imagery from Seattle, I reminded them of the city's charms and told them to let me know if they were going to return.

Late in January, the Seattle Seahawks were in the homestretch of what would be their magical and historic year. It was a surreal, pinch-me-is-this-really-happening moment for Seattle. Our fans were tough customers—accustomed to "close-but-not-quite" results from their professional sports teams. Many were jaded, afraid to believe, and weary from so many losses. It was hard to fathom that our team was actually going to the Super Bowl.

The city was over the moon with excitement, and it seemed everyone was in a good mood. Or maybe it was a sugar high—ever since running back Marshawn Lynch started eating Skittles on the sidelines in celebration of big plays, sales of the rainbow-colored candies went through the roof in Seattle! By the time Super Bowl Sunday rolled around, it was next to impossible to get your hands on a bag of them.

A week before the big game, I got a Facebook message from Culler saying she and Roxanne wanted to come to Seattle for the game. I chuckled a little and messaged her back, saying, "You *do* know that the Super Bowl is taking place in New Jersey and not Seattle, right?" She said that of course they were aware of this but really wanted to be in Seattle when the city clinched its historic Super Bowl victory.

They were confident the Hawks were going to win. So much so that they bought last-minute airplane tickets and traveled all day, arriving just in time to see the big game. Culler and Roxanne were firm in their decision to move to Seattle someday soon, and they knew this game was going to be an important moment in the city's history. They hoped it might also be an exciting beginning to their own history in Seattle. It was the dead of winter, and the lodging season was quiet in my house, so I invited them to stay with me again.

Becoming an innkeeper and excelling at the professional aspects of having guests in your home non-stop makes entertaining friends and family a breeze. You're ready for guests anytime. Since I have the luxury of two extra bedrooms and two full baths, it's hard to say no when friends or family ask if they can stay at my place.

I now have a number of friends in Seattle that are also Airbnb hosts, and I know some of them charge friends and family to stay in their home. I sense that they are so used to seeing their extra rooms as revenue generators that they can't separate that fact from the idea that in the old days, no one would ever charge someone to be a guest in their home. This is, of course, something each host is going to have to work out personally. I think it's gauche to charge friends and family. Since Culler and Roxanne had become friends, their second stay in my home was free.

And you know what? The weekend the Seahawks won, wowing a city that had grown accustomed to being sports losers despite excelling at everything else, I knew I was forging a bond with two women I hope to know for life.

In the minutes after the Seahawks crushed the Denver Broncos 43–8, we took to the streets of Capitol Hill's Pike-Pine corridor to celebrate the win with thousands of other awestruck fans. We drank champagne, we sprayed champagne, and we danced with each other and with strangers. Skittles rained down around us and crunched below our feet as people around us tossed handfuls of the candies high in the air. Our clothes and hair were soaked in bubbly, we high-fived and hugged and laughed and laughed. It was a moment I will never forget and one I will forever treasure. Not just because of the win.

As I approached the one-year mark on my Airbnb journey, I contacted Culler and Roxanne and told them I was coming to Knoxville. Their invitation for me to come stay with them, extended that memorable Super Bowl weekend, wasn't the first I'd received from guests. I have open invitations to stay in Belgium, Avignon, Paris, San Francisco, and Sonoma, and I'm sure there will be more in the future. These invitations are an unexpected side benefit of opening my house to guests.

Except they're no longer just my former guests, they've become friends. I never expected that by opening my doors to strangers, I would open myself to friendships with people I'd never meet under typical circumstances.

Fate is a funny thing. You never know how that person who bumps into you at the train station, chases after you with your left-behind umbrella, or buys you a cup of coffee when they're in line in front of you just to be nice is going to change your life. Strangers change my life every week. It was John Steinbeck who wisely said, "When two people meet, each one is changed by the other so you've got two new people."

I'd like to believe it was fate that brought me to the low place I'd found myself in during the spring of 2013. At the time, my choice was to sink further into despair, or rise to the opportunity Jeff's move offered me. In my wildest imagination, I could never have forecasted the strange series of events that led up to that life-changing call and my subsequent move.

As I enter the final months of this first year of hosting, I am floored and humbled by the amazing people who have literally walked into my life…and chosen to remain. Unlike the Seattle Freeze I experience with new acquaintances and even many of my longtime friends, I find my exchanges with Culler and Roxanne drawing us closer and closer. In part because we are willing and open, but also because we expend the effort. Sometimes you have to work for the things you really want.

If the Seahawks could defy history and win a Super Bowl, I have no doubt I can defy the chilly Seattle tendencies that have shaped me and jaded me in this Emerald City. To dare to believe that I can write a better personal history for myself.

FAIRBANKS

3.29.13

"Hello!" he exuberantly calls up the stairs. Standing in the kitchen, I hear him removing his shoes in the foyer below the hall stairs. "Hi! How was work?" I shout back, continuing to chop the dinner vegetables. David, an attractive 49-year-old with gray-blonde hair, tops the stairs and approaches the kitchen, an expensive North Face carry-on bag in his hands. "Work was good. But look what I got tonight at REI!" He unzips the sleek black bag and shows me its interior pockets and extender handle. "Back in Fairbanks, we don't have REIs quite as awesome as yours." His face beams like a little boy's.

David's a boat chief for a large fishing vessel, working a two-week stint at the local Fisherman's Terminal. He booked his stay with me the very night he learned of Airbnb from a coworker. David's friendlier than most; he calls me from the grocery store to see if I need anything, or texts me while I'm at the gym to let me know he's made extra food for dinner and hopes I'm hungry. He's the epitome of kindness laid bare, belly up and exposed in all its fundamental human decency. It's both sweet and a little disconcerting. In my heart of hearts, I want to believe there are people in this world that are kind for no reason. But as a single woman, I am often wary of a man's intentions when he acts a little *too* friendly.

Thankfully, David talks a lot about his fiancée Stephanie, and I can tell by the way he talks about her that he's in love. They've been engaged for two years, and though a wedding date has not yet been set, he already wears a titanium wedding ring on his left ring finger. After show-and-tell on the carry-on bag, David proudly holds up two pairs of dark purple, spandex workout leggings he bought for Stephanie. He knows she'll like watching TV in them or wearing them on their weekend hikes. "What a lovely, practical souvenir from Seattle," I say, once again internally noting his sweet thoughtfulness.

When David is home in Fairbanks, he and Stephanie like to frequent karaoke bars. Both non-drinkers, they always leave before midnight, when the "natives and kids" are prone to act out their alcohol-fueled scenes. In the evenings, after dinner, the couple smokes together over their Jenn-Air cooktop. The fumes disappear into the stove's down-draft vent—a feature so effective, people have no idea they smoke indoors. So David says, as he steps outside to smoke on my Juliet balcony.

Smoking is something many hosts have an issue with, and it's their decision as to whether they'll allow it in their home. I don't allow it *in* my home, but I do allow guests to light up on the two, main-floor balconies and in the back yard. I find that many of my European guests smoke, and they appreciate my lax policy about it.

All of my guests have been respectful about using ashtrays and disposing of their cigarette butts. One woman from Omaha even generously offered to bring her own ashtray from home! When I read her message, I had an instant visual of her carefully wrapping an ashtray in bubble wrap and placing it in her carry-on bag. I assured her I would gladly make a couple ashtrays available and that it wasn't necessary for her to bring one. I think she appreciated my casual attitude about smoking, because nowadays most people have a huge problem with it. She's now been a two-time visitor to my home and one of my most conscientious guests.

David speaks often of his aging parents, who live in Illinois. He says they're amazingly fit and still play tennis twice a week at their country club, though his 89-year-old father suffers from Alzheimer's. David recalled one occasion when his entire family was home for the holidays and they heard a knock at the front door. The paramedics standing on the porch told them their father had called 911, complaining of chest pains. Due to his short-term memory loss, their dad had failed to inform the family about the call. Watching their father, a former neuroscientist and esteemed professor, deteriorate via the organ he studied his entire career, has been particularly disturbing to David and his family.

David is grateful that his two-weeks-on, two-weeks-off shifts on the boat allow him to get back to Illinois fairly often. But not regularly enough. He is keenly aware that his time with his parents is limited, though he's comforted that his seven siblings help his parents and do their best to keep him apprised of what's happening back home.

David's stories remind me of a Norman Rockwell painting. I picture Stephanie in her purple leggings, huddled with David over the cooktop, heads bent toward one another as they share a secret smoke. I can see his big Catholic family about to sit down for holiday supper—napkins on laps and heads bowed, poised to give thanks—and imagine the bewildered paramedic standing outside the front door, a hand raised in a tentative knock. A capture of everyday life in all its intricately beautiful mundanity. The stories are a souvenir for my mind, unknowingly gifted by my most memorable guests.

I'll leave you with the image of David and me, unlikely dinner companions who'd never connect in "real life," standing over our plates at my kitchen countertop, swapping stories like we shared food.

FULL CIRCLE

4.8.14

My leg was extended high in front of me on the wooden bar, and as I bent forward to grab the underside of my foot to stretch my hamstring, I was startled by the sound of another foot landing with a thud, just inches from mine. There was no grace in the movement and I, in my don't-look-anyone-in-the-eye-at-the-gym mindset, didn't even see the woman approach.

She plunked her foot awkwardly and aggressively on the bar, paying no heed to the implied social rules of the gym that demand you stay in your own space and ignore the fact that everyone is sweating and scantily dressed. Given the sudden intrusion into my personal bubble, I was forced to turn and actually look at her. I'm not sure what I expected, but when I saw her huge, almond-shaped brown eyes and her wide smile, I laughed, in delayed recognition of my houseguest. Her action on the bar, devoid of grace and composure, was particularly hilarious because she gets paid to be elegant and on point. Vita was staying with me for one month while on tour with Disney's production of *The Lion King*.

She breezed into town late on a Sunday night, fresh off the plane from a month of touring with the show in Hawaii. When I saw her standing in the driveway, bewildered and lost amid a pile of luggage, I could feel in my gut she was going to be one of my more unique visitors. She fumbled with her phone, trying to find my address so she'd know which door was mine. She wore a neon blue trucker's hat emblazoned with "Hawaii" across the top, leather coat, skinny jeans, pink wedge tennis shoes, and a huge smile. Her outfit was sort of Miami-meets-Milan—all dead giveaways that this beautiful woman was not from around these parts. Color *and* fashion? Be still my Seattle, black-clad, wears-socks-with-Birkenstocks heart.

Vita, apparently caught up in packing and the mechanics involved in a large-scale theatrical production on the move, didn't see the reminder email about her reservation. Airbnb sends itinerary messages to guests and hosts 24 hours before check-in to alert both parties that a booking is confirmed for the next day. It's a great opportunity for guests and hosts to connect about arrival times and any last-minute details. However, I have found a lot of people dismiss the reminders, or never see them at all.

Hosts are guilty of this too. I've heard horror stories from friends who had shown up for bookings in far-flung countries, only to find their hosts had completely forgotten they were coming. One Icelandic woman even had to kick her brother-in-law out of bed in his bathrobe so she could make up the spare room for my friends. Like many things in life, it's not a perfect system, but it works well most of the time.

Vita had messaged me her arrival time a while back, but she'd clearly missed the check-in details and key box instructions. Since guests can use the door code to come in at their leisure, I don't stress over arrival times. I'm happy to store guests' bags in the garage or living room if they arrive early in the day before their room is ready at 3:00 p.m., or if another guest is checking in and the departing guest has a later flight. If I'm expecting a guest at a really late hour and they are staying for a long duration (like Vita was) I make it a point to stay up late to welcome them in person and get them situated in their room.

Within a half hour of her arrival, Vita came up to my bedroom and quietly knocked on the door. I cautiously peered out. As my eyes adjusted to the dark hallway, I saw the outline of her petite frame, standing there in adorable footie pajamas. She sheepishly admitted to locking herself out of her room and hoped I had an extra key. I hide spare keys for each room all over the house so if a guest texts me or comes to me in a lock-out situation, I can easily tell them where to find their room's spare key. It's happened numerous times. Lamp bases and dictionaries make for convenient and accessible hiding places that aren't too obvious.

After that initial late-night awkwardness, I secretly worried Vita was going to be a high-maintenance guest. Since she was a high-caliber performer, I feared she might turn out to be bit of a diva. But her beaming smile and friendly vibe assuaged my fears and it felt natural to want to accommodate her.

Vita and I fell into a natural rhythm during her stay. Her days were filled with yoga classes, the gym, and massages to keep her body in top performing condition. A theater performer's workday extends far beyond the few hours of a show. We'd often run into each other at the gym, and then meet again later at the house after our workouts. Standing at the kitchen countertop, chatting in our sweaty workout clothes, we'd sneak diet-killer donut holes and laugh good-naturedly about the cute gay boys at the gym who never paid us any attention. We'd also share stories about our families and childhood.

When she was young, Vita loved taking jazz and tap classes, but her mom insisted she also take ballet. Her mother thought it was vital that she learn grace and refinement in her movements, not just how to dance. "But I don't want to! Why are you making me?" she would moan to her mother in a tortured-sounding voice. And her mother's reply, one muttered over and over by mothers everywhere was, "Because you'll thank me for it later." Little-girl Vita would stomp around and groan some more, then grab her pink tutu off its hook, and with her head bent, dejectedly follow her mother out the door to go to class.

Fast forward twenty years to a casting call from Disney looking for a performer with a particular look, who had tap, jazz, *and* ballet skills. Vita recalled those tedious ballet classes with a laugh, and was sure to thank her mother when she landed the part on Broadway. Later, she transitioned to touring worldwide.

When I told friends I was hosting a member of this prestigious musical in my home for a month, they were impressed. People were always curious about who was staying in my home, but because the Disney show was so famous, this guest was of particular interest. When I told friends that Vita had offered me two tickets to the show and a backstage tour, they were wowed. One more perk this hosting gig had unexpectedly brought into my life.

Over time, as my friends and online acquaintances got used to hearing more about my interactions with guests, like the invites to stay abroad and the perks associated with unusual people like Vita, I began to notice a shift. Both in myself and in my friends. As my level of comfort with hosting deepened and my friends' familiarity with my hosting gig grew, my stories began to feel less strange and more natural—as if society could actually work this way for the long term, in this new frontier of the home-sharing economy. If we allow ourselves to get over our fears and prejudices of one another, it's surprising and gratifying to see how fruitful life can become. It's a new way of life that has a remarkable way of creating community and widening horizons.

After visiting Vita at the theater and seeing things up close, I could tell people lots of interesting tidbits from backstage—how the performers' costumes are housed on a pulley, rotisserie-style, so they can just slip them on between acts, and how the costume designers get the lioness's tears to work—but to me, those details weren't nearly as interesting as my experience meeting Vita and having the pleasure of getting to know her for a month.

It occurred to me during Vita's stay that I was more impressed by her as a person than I was by the excitement of her career. On the first anniversary of my becoming a host, Vita was there. The final guest of my first year, and a fitting reminder that people are often so much more than we think they are on first glance, based on a stereotype or projection. I remembered that first night we met, when I feared she would be a diva. She turned out to be one of the most down-to-earth people I hosted in the house all year.

The evening Vita checked out, she left me a bouquet of flowers with a note of thanks and a gift certificate for a one-hour massage. Days after arriving in Seattle, she'd received word from Disney they wanted her to return to Broadway. When she learned I would soon be traveling to New York City, she promised to invite me to another performance and connect with me after the show. I'll be seeing her this summer.

I began the spring of 2013 in a depressed, scared, and desperate state. But after only one year of opening my house and my heart to strangers, my world had grown so wide. It was fitting that Vita and Disney's song, *The Circle of Life* were on my mind as I closed out that first year.

It's the circle of life and it moves us all
Through despair and hope, through faith and love
Till we find our place, on the path unwinding
In the circle, the circle of life

Things in my life now felt secure and bountiful. It had been the most memorable year of my life—all because I decided to meet my fears head-on and allow people in.

COMING HOME

June, 2014

You, dear Reader, are the final guest in this story. I hope I've offered you tips and insight into the world of hosting, but also allowed you in.

The nature of sharing a first-person account gave me pause each time I committed a person or an experience to the page. Was this true? Was that really how things happened? When reporting as a journalist, it's imperative your writing is objective and factual, but writing a memoir allows an author to share as liberally as their heart, head, and memory have the stamina for.

There's nothing like diminished boundaries and repeated contact with strangers in one's home to really put a person face-to-face with her physical vulnerability and limitations. In addition to that vulnerable physical space, I spent most of 2013 and early 2014 in an exposed space emotionally. I was open to the lessons my guests were teaching me, and my experiences as a host reconfirmed again and again that I had developed a new worldview—one that rocked my interior foundation and changed me on a core level. It is the only reason you're reading these words today.

I admit that throughout these pages, I often paused, wondering how to accurately chronicle the true series of events that had taken place in my home, while giving respectful insight into to the real people who inspired the stories. It's my writerly way and inherent nature to be the participant-observer, mentally taking notes and scribbling down key phrases from guests—hoping to weave the pieces into stories later. It's always been more comfortable for me to shine a light on someone else than on myself. "Look with me, not at me," I often say.

Ironically, in a book about letting people in, I knew I was holding many parts of myself back in an effort to be informative—rarely showing my full emotional hand.

What I didn't overtly bring to the story in some of the prior pages, I'll share with you now. The person who opened up her home to strangers on April 3, 2013? She's gone. She'd come unmoored from herself when she met Grayson and was drowning when he left; somewhere along the way in her first year of hosting, she drifted away for good.

After I took on the challenge of moving, and opening my home to complete strangers, I knew it was time to face my next emotional and financial challenge—therapy. I had contemplated how the expense of therapy could potentially crush me, but the alternative would probably have set me up for a lifetime of performing far below my potential. I knew I had to make the investment in myself and my future.

I began attending weekly therapy sessions in June of 2013, and by using examples from some of the conversations and encounters I was having in my home and personal life, I was able to work through a lot of issues that I now realized had held me back for a couple decades. Things like repeatedly choosing narcissistic, emotionally unavailable men; not trusting myself and my life choices; failing to recognize my self-worth; and undiagnosed anxiety—just to name a few "small" issues.

As I worked through the often-painful process of therapy, I noticed that the rent I wasn't paying to live in my home (because my Airbnb income supported the entire rent and then some) allowed me to pay cash out of pocket for therapy. Therapy allowed me to say goodbye to my former self, and helped the new me arrive home—to myself.

Though I am still a recovering people-pleaser who struggles with occasional bouts of anxiety, I am now confident I can handle anything that life throws my way. Looking back on my first year of hosting, I find it amazing what I accomplished. I rose from the depths of my depressed emotional and financial state in early 2013 and built a business from scratch, and I was far more successful at it than I ever dreamed I'd be—even in my most optimistic projections. Meeting and befriending generous, beautiful people from around the world—all 122 of them in my first year!—was an added benefit. Hosting on Airbnb delivered unexpected, intangible daily gifts which even today continue to unfold and amaze me.

If any of this resonates with you—maybe you're a person curious about hosting strangers or perhaps you're hoping to make changes in your life and in your relationships to "let people in," I encourage you to be brave and test the waters of that vulnerable place inside you. Believe me, it's worth it.

Trust yourself and what you have to offer, then watch how the world rises up to meet you.

ACKNOWLEDGMENTS

When I was working in real estate, my friend Carla Valente told me I would one day write a book. I was afraid to believe her prediction, but I secretly wished she was right. After my editor finished revisions on the book, Carla was one of my first readers, and I am humbled by her endless support as a friend and confidante.

The seed of an idea for this story was planted somewhere around the two-month-mark of my journey as an Airbnb host. It wasn't until I had completed that first year and was over-indulging in an ambling pub crawl with my friend Billy Grdanski that I really believed I had a story people might be interested in reading. Billy supported me wholeheartedly and was my cheerleader that day and always. I am forever grateful for his unwavering support of my writing and our decade-long friendship. After the book was written, my editor Sara Addicott became my lifeline. She helped me when I was lost and couldn't quite find my way around my story. Like any good editor, she gently guided me and helped me get out of my own way and believe in the value of my experiences. I am forever grateful for her intellect, skill, and hand-holding. My travel partner and talented friend, Michelle McCartney, did the whimsical illustration for the cover, and I love how she captured Seattle as another character in the book. Char Davidson was my graphic design savior when it came to finishing the design details for the book's hard copy release. Her friendship, support, and "fake it 'til you make it" advice has bolstered my freelance career and saved me from returning to a 9-5 job. Bee Tangsurat is an editor colleague of mine, who has advanced her skills to include book formatting; I was fortunate she was willing to join my team. To all of my first readers, including my final reader, Johnny Miller—thank you. Everyone offered such wonderful insight and feedback, and they really enhanced the story.

Life is an amazing adventure. I can't wait to see what's next.

* * *

"In travel writing there's the story you're sent to report and then there's the story behind the scenes, and the latter is always vastly more interesting." -Andrew McCarthy

ABOUT THE AUTHOR

Rochelle Short is a freelance writer, editor, and social media consultant. She continues to host people from around the world in her home in the Capitol Hill neighborhood of Seattle, Washington.

When she's not acting like a tourist in her own town, she enjoys traveling the globe and is presently working on her next book. Rochelle welcomes the chance to connect with you! Find her online and on social media at:

- www.lettingpeoplein.com
- Instagram and Twitter: @typeaseattle
- Facebook: www.facebook.com/RochelleShortAuthor

If Rochelle's story has piqued your interest in signing up for Airbnb, please connect to the site via the following link and let them know she sent you! www.airbnb.com/c /rshort

Made in the USA
San Bernardino, CA
12 November 2014